Praise for *Invasion of the Dead*

"Brian Blount's book on the impor[illegible]tology for understanding the gospel message combines in a winning and profound way a scholar's careful historical analysis of the biblical texts with a preacher's vivid articulation of the issues at stake for our world and our time. Blount's attempt to reclaim and to reinvigorate the apocalyptic worldview found in the New Testament for preaching in the contemporary American context succeeds masterfully."

—MARTINUS C. DE BOER, Professor of New Testament, Vrije Universiteit, Amsterdam

"The word 'apocalyptic' sends many readers of Scripture into flight; but not Brian Blount, who knows both that apocalyptic theology is central to the New Testament and that popular culture reveals an obsession with apocalyptic scenarios. *Invasion of the Dead* takes up the book of Revelation, the Letters of Paul, and the Gospel of Mark and weaves a provocative conversation with both secular culture and the dispirited culture of American Christianity. The result is genuinely apocalyptic proclamation—a word that is convicting, energizing, and profoundly hopeful. This goes on the required reading list!"

—BEVERLY R. GAVENTA, Distinguished Professor of New Testament Interpretation, Baylor University

"This is, quite simply, a stunning book on resurrection, the deepest mystery and the boldest claim of the Christian gospel. Brian Blount is a master biblical interpreter, but here he shows himself equally gifted at theological inquiry and cultural analysis. The result is that he not only recovers a compelling biblical vision of resurrection for today, he also knocks off centuries of rust in the church's misunderstanding and enables the resurrection to shine again as the invasion of God's power into a world occupied and preoccupied with death."

—THOMAS G. LONG, Bandy Professor of Preaching at Candler School of Theology

"These lectures are as electrifying to read as they were when I first heard them spoken. With the eloquence and passion of an apocalyptic prophet, Brian Blount walks into the heart of a culture obsessed with death and celebrates God's 'silver bullet' in defeating it: resurrection. He takes us to the very heart of Christian faith and challenges us to believe it and preach it. Best of all, he models how to do so."

—NORA TUBBS TISDALE, Clement-Muehl Professor of Homiletics, Yale Divinity School

"Brian Blount has written a life-giving, faith-building work that will revitalize not only preachers but also any thoughtful Christian willing to wrestle with how the cross has been misinterpreted and employed for abusive ends. His book is especially timely in a world where religion, including much of what passes for Christianity, colludes with violent and destructive powers. Blount confronts the pathologies of faith and preaching that have incubated in death and sin, and audaciously claims the healing possibilities that are opened through the resurrection of Jesus Christ."

—THOMAS H. TROEGER, Lantz Professor of Christian Communication, Yale Divinity School and Institute of Sacred Music

Invasion of the Dead

Invasion of the Dead

Preaching Resurrection

Brian K. Blount

First edition
Published by Westminster John Knox Press
Louisville, Kentucky

14 15 16 17 18 19 20 21 22 23—10 9 8 7 6 5 4 3 2 1

Book design by Drew Stevens
Cover design by Eric Walljasper, Minneapolis, MN
Cover illustration: Cemetery in fog in autumn by Aleksey Stemmer © shutterstock.com

Library of Congress Cataloging-in-Publication Data

Blount, Brian K., 1955–
Invasion of the dead : preaching resurrection / Brian K. Blount.—First edition.
pages cm
ISBN 978-0-664-23941-1 (alk. paper)
1. Jesus Christ—Resurrection. 2. Preaching. 3. Jesus Christ—Resurrection—Sermons. I. Title.
BT482.B56 2014
232'.5—dc23

2013041170

For Loved Ones lost . . .
and one day found

Contents

Acknowledgments ix
Introduction: Invasion of the Dead xi

Chapter 1: Dawn of the Dead: Preaching the Apocalypse 1
Chapter 2: Call of Duty: A Sermon 33
Chapter 3: Preaching Paul: Apocalyptic Vulnerability 44
Chapter 4: Raise the Dead: A Sermon 70
Chapter 5: Preaching Mark: Invasion of the Dead 80
Chapter 6: Rise! A Sermon 109

Notes 121

Acknowledgments

When Harry Attridge, at the time Dean of the Yale University Divinity School, shared with me the Divinity School's invitation to be the 2011 Lyman Beecher Lecturer, I initially feared that the duties associated with my position as President of Union Presbyterian Seminary would prevent my acceptance. I was, and remain, ever so grateful to Dean Attridge and the Yale Divinity Faculty for this wonderful opportunity. I am particularly grateful to Professor Nora Tubbs Tisdale, my former colleague and writing partner, who greeted my wife and me so warmly upon our arrival in New Haven and encouraged colleagues and students to attend my lectures. Indeed, everyone at Yale was incredibly hospitable and received me with a generosity of spirit and collegiality.

I am especially grateful to the Board of Trustees at Union Presbyterian Seminary who allayed my fears about accepting the Yale invitation by promising to give me the support and the time I needed to do the research and writing necessary to draft my lectures. I single out particularly the Rev. Dr. Art Ross, chair of the Board of Trustees at the time, and William L. Rikard, current chair of the Board of Trustees. Both gentlemen encouraged me to accept the lectures as a way to further my scholarship and, by doing so, to represent in the very endeavor Union Presbyterian Seminary's commitment to providing the space necessary for its faculty and even administrators to do strong research and writing. Art's words, "You need to do this, and we need to provide you with the resources to make it possible for you to do this," convinced me finally to accept the Yale Divinity Faculty's invitation.

I would also like to thank all of the Trustees of Union Presbyterian Seminary who journeyed with me to New Haven to represent the school and provide "moral support." It is always delightful when traveling to have members of the home team travel along. The Reverends Arthur Ross III, Robert E. Dunham, Edward A. McLeod Jr., Ernest T. Thompson III, Alexander W. Evans, and Jim Holderness; plus lay trustees William L. Rikard, Lillian James Smith, Ginny Ward Holderness, and Anne Jones Logan, MD—all were a tonic to my spirit throughout. I am also very grateful to retired Union Presbyterian Seminary Professor Ron Byars and his wife, Susan, for also journeying from Kentucky to show their support. I am equally indebted to the Reverends Gary W. Charles and Michael E. Livingston, who read early drafts of the lectures and provided invaluable feedback.

Finally, I am grateful to David Maxwell, editor at Westminster John Knox Press, for attending the lectures and encouraging me to transform them into a publication. I hope that you, the reader, find it a useful resource.

Introduction

Invasion of the Dead

I did not begin with resurrection. Who does? Except, perhaps, during the Easter season. The Gospels do not even begin there. In the earliest, Mark, Jesus gets to the subject only after his narrative journey is half over (8:31). He reconsiders it infrequently (9:31; 10:34; 14:28), perhaps because his audience seems incapable of comprehending (9:10), not to mention believing it (12:18–27). In the end, completely baffled by it, what is left of his discipleship corps runs away from it (16:6–8). As we follow the Gospels' lead, it is no surprise that, though resurrection is arguably the most important element of our faith (1 Cor. 15:14), all too often we take much time, energy, and striving to get to it, too. Babies must be born. Children must grow. Young adults must journey. Families must bond. Careers must blossom. Temptations must appear. Trouble must threaten. Crosses must be carried. Victories must be won. Death must be endured. And yet, still we hesitate. Anxiously, desperately, even incredulously, we contemplate and reconsider resurrection. It is as much our destination as it is our destiny. But the rigors of the journey to it divert our attention and shift our focus until what troubles us here overwhelms what promises us there.

Like exasperated parents, on a tempestuously long, arduously winding road trip, trapped in a steamy, sweaty car jammed with luggage, snacks, and physically pent-up and emotionally stirred-up children, we dissuade attention on and questions about the destination lest the fervor over being there wrecks the process of getting there. Stop thinking about it. Stop asking about it. Stop obsessing over it. "We'll get there when we get there!" Some time right after Good Friday. So, put your focus on Good Friday. Divert your attention to Good Friday.

After all, we Christians are a people of the cross. The cross marks us. Identifies us. The cross is our brand. Oddly enough, considering what the cross represents, it is our comfortable place of being. We luxuriate in its symbolism of suffering. As surely as the McDonald's arches signal the site of burgers and fries, so the cross signals the location of a Christian community or a Christian believer. As we are what we eat, so we are what we wear. In our case, it is death. We, therefore, whether in our preaching and teaching, our living and learning, our striving and struggling, endeavor to get to Calvary as fast as we can and linger there as long as we are able. With all this dying to be done, heaven can wait.

To be sure, the Christian conception of the cross is the reimagining of death. As the apostle Paul notes, God takes what humans intend to be the definitive act of disfigurement and dishonor and reclaims it as something uniquely revelatory. Capital punishment. Death. On a cross. The end of a life that reveals the meaning of life. In that case, the cross is the consummate act of divine irony. What the Romans believed to be the cessation of life and meaning, God claims as the marker that defines the possibilities of life for all of us, for all of time. The cross, then, becomes the ultimate apocalypse: the revelation of God's intention for humankind. Through struggle and even death, God reveals life.

In my Beecher lectures, I wanted to reveal something clarifying about our death-obsessed, apocalyptic eschatology. Specifically, after explaining apocalyptic eschatology as a key component of first-century popular culture, I aimed to consider how apocalyptic eschatology might be biblically reclaimed and theologically reconfigured for preaching in our contemporary American context. I therefore started with Jesus' trial and execution, added in the Gospel portrayals of Jesus' life and ministry, expanded out to Paul's ruminations about the crucified and risen Christ, drew in John of Patmos's prophetic disclosures about the slaughtered Lamb, and situated all of that within the eschatological environment of the first-century Greco-Roman world that was the New Testament writers' field of operation.

I intended to craft lectures that would help preachers more effectively proclaim apocalyptic eschatology for our time. My focusing question was this: How can we reveal the hope of transcendent life in the midst of ever-present death? There is a supplemental operational question: Is the cross the right revelatory mechanism? It is for Christians. Is it not?

During my research, I slowly and somewhat begrudgingly came to two reorienting conclusions. First, and significantly (at least for me), I did not need to interpret apocalyptic eschatology in a way that made it more accessible to individuals and communities in our time. At least not secular individuals and communities. And I did not need, during the Beecher Lectures on Preaching, to exhort American preachers to so interpret it either. To be sure, several of the scholars whom I admire greatly were, in their writings, doing just that. J. Christiaan Beker, my former teacher, friend, and teaching colleague, makes the powerful case that apocalyptic eschatology is so crucial to the formation of the Jesus movement and the Pauline churches it birthed that if we attempt, existentially or otherwise, to interpret apocalyptic sensibility out of our contemporary Christian proclamation, we are left with nothing like the faith that the biblical writers intended to bequeath us.[1] Even so, he painfully observes, contemporary Christian thinkers and preachers have either mangled (in sectarian views) apocalyptic eschatology or left it for dead (in mainstream views). Beker calls upon biblical interpreters and preachers to reclaim apocalyptic eschatology as a, or perhaps *the,* fundamental predisposition of Christian theology. He demands that we resurrect it. In my Beecher lectures, I was determined to join those scholars who have championed that cause, find a place in the front of the lineup of folks determined to redeem apocalyptic eschatology's place in theological and cultural conversation.

I came to realize that the front was actually rather crowded—not by biblical interpreters, theologians, and preachers, but by the people who drive secular popular culture.

Contemporary artists, writers, directors, and producers of American popular culture are already offering and interpreting apocalyptic scenarios in vastly entertaining and terrifyingly convincing ways. Like us Christian interpreters, the interpreters of contemporary American popular culture appear obsessed with the ever-present and all-encompassing nature of death. For popular-culture artists, too, death is revelatory. Death reveals the fragility and tenderness of life, but not necessarily its transcendence. In fact, in the imagery of popular culture, it is death that appears transcendent. Life trembles before it and struggles to endure it. All too often, life seems incapable of defeating death. Though there is that hope. Such hope, that what is good about life can overcome what is destructive about death, provides the dramatic lure, the proverbial carrot on a dramatic stick that hooks readers of novels and viewers of film. They keep coming back because they keep believing that sooner or later the death-wielding vampires, werewolves, zombies, aliens, pandemics, environmental disasters, and the horrifying devastation they bring with them—all such will themselves die, and life will win out.

This initial research recognition caused me some concern. If apocalyptic eschatology is already being interpreted in a highly effective manner in the works of popular culture, is it really important that my lectures call preachers to the task of reclaiming and reinterpreting apocalyptic eschatology for our times? Our time seems already focused on my task. And, compared with preachers and their pulpits, the popular-culture interpreters of our time have larger audiences to reach and better communicative tools with which to reach them.

That is when my second reorienting conclusion kicked in. I was caught up with the reflection that popular culture and popular Christianity are both mesmerized by death and dying. Both appear to believe that one can only arrive at life by driving through death, that one can only understand life if one comprehends death, that transcendent life is integrally bound up with the ever-present-ness of death. Just as Jesus' death on that Roman cross clarifies everything about human life and living, so the death of the planet to the living dead or the environmental cataclysm refreshes and refocuses our understanding of what it means to be alive. My second reorienting conclusion interrupted my thesis thinking at just this point. Even though Jesus' apparent march to the cross and his devastating death on the cross occupy almost all the energy and space of the gospel story, nagging at me was the thought that there was an apocalyptic moment whose revelatory power and promise trumped even that spectacular death. That moment lies on the backside of the cross, way down in the weeds of the postclimactic and perhaps even anticlimactic denouement of the Jesus story.

Resurrection.

Here, it seemed to me, was an apocalyptic eschatological moment of biblical proportions that popular culture does not fully or rightly engage. Even Christianity appears to restrict its engagement with resurrection to the season of Easter, now rationally tricked out with accessible metaphors of life renewed in the vibrant colors, tasteful meal traditions, and acceptable bunny/egg mythology of spring. The shock of the thing is dulled by its trailing position to and its narrative comparison with the traumatic scandal of the cross. Its historical veracity is diminished by its reckless implausibility. And yet, if one is questing for a pure moment of apocalypse, where a divine prerogative wrecks the principles of natural and physical existence, where the intention for life is revealed not by death but by life itself, the answer lies with resurrection. Anyone arbitrarily forced to make a stand on a single piece of revelatory Christian ground that explains the essential purpose of the faith would, it seems to me, have to stake a claim to the property where God staged Jesus' resurrection. Not Golgotha. The graveyard is the place you want to be. The reclaiming of a withering corpse and the reconstituting of a departed spirit is the thing you want to see. If something crazy does not happen in the graveyard, the meaning of whatever happened on Golgotha is diminished. A hero, even a martyr, will have died, but not the agent of God designated to reveal the truth about life. Not unless, no matter the manner of dying, after dying, in spite of dying, *Jesus lives.*

Using life to reveal the meaning of life does not have the dramatic flair (or believable plotting) of working with death.

Perhaps that is why popular culture and Christian tradition focus on death. The more spectacular the death, the better. It is as though the more gruesome dying is, the more clarified our appreciation of life becomes. So the zombies devour, the vampires bite, the werewolves ravage, the floods despoil, the earthquakes crush, the aliens conquer, the crosses crucify—and when the book is finished or the movie is ended, our view of life is refreshed, renewed with a grander sense of appreciation for what we have too often taken for granted. The apocalyptic moment, directed by death, reveals the beauty of a life we had best, sooner than later, cherish and respect. Jesus' death brings a similar sigh of existential relief. The horror he endured was owed to us. The fact that God allows us to escape it by turning it upon Jesus in our stead reveals to us just how special God considers us to be. That substitutionary maneuver calls upon us, sooner rather than later, to cherish and respect this life and those who populate it with us. One can use death like this because it is real, it is tangible. In a world as mangled as ours, death is always believable.

Resurrection, though, requires a spectacular suspension of belief. Even in popular culture, where suspension of belief is commonly requested and regularly conceded, not even the undead (e.g., vampire, zombie) really live again. They are, after all, only undead. Life is not a negative; it is the ultimate positive. Resurrection *is* Life. But once the negation of death sets in, there is no rationally justifiable means of getting back on the credit side of the existential ledger. Not unless you are God and Jesus three days after his agonizing death on that Roman cross. According to all the canonical Gospel sources, the one-time messianic corpse is not undead. *Jesus lives.* He does not live with the restraints that shackle the rest of us to the logic of dying and the reality of death. He lives positively free from every restraint. And he lives forever. His living does not just conquer death in a singularly miraculous moment; his living reconfigures the physics of death and portends death's impending demise. For all of us.

It is Jesus' life, then, that reveals the ultimate meaning of life. Resurrection is the quintessential apocalyptic moment.

And so, my apocalyptic focus turned away from historical cataclysm, destruction, and death, even death on that Roman cross, to the eschatological capitalization of Life. I worked on suspending belief in order to shore up my faith that Mark's empty tomb had opened itself to something stupefyingly irregular. It was that irregularity that captured my attention and thereby became the focus for my Beecher lectures.

These lectures/essays explore the portrait and meaning of resurrection through three canonical New Testament lenses: the book of Revelation, the Letters of Paul, the Gospel of Mark. Because they are the Lyman Beecher Lectures on Preaching, I follow each lecture with a sermon that explores the preceding lecture's thesis. Each sermon has been proclaimed before a live (as opposed to undead) congregation. I enter the context for each sermon in a small paragraph at the opening of each of the three preaching sections.

In the lectures and the sermons, my goal is to reverse the apocalyptic logic that typically regulates our living and reveals the essence of our being. We look through the prism of death and pray that, through all the confusion and clutter, we can find the meaning of life. I start with a clear shot of life, marvel at how that life engages and obliterates death, and in the process of that annihilation, reveals life's essence and purpose. I end up with resurrection.

Chapter 1
Dawn of the Dead
Preaching the Apocalypse

Resurrection is a weapon. It is not vindication for a life, wrongly terminated. It is reinstigation for a battle, rightly fought. It is not the anticlimax that shadows God's crowning achievement on the cross. It is the shot that reignites a fiery engagement between forces claiming lordship over creation. It is not about a man. It is about a war.

Resurrection is a weapon. Indeed, in the cosmic conflict where the Almighty and Creator God, who has no equal, is found inexplicably engaged by the forces of satanic Sin and hellish Death, resurrection is *the* weapon. The stakes are nothing less than life and its complete and eternal loss. To win, God must detonate a force as ferocious for life as God's enemies are vicious for death.

Wielding the sword of slaughter and the crossbow of crucifixion, Sin and Death are poised for the most stunning of victories. Unless God can unleash an even greater, opposing power. On the violent and unforgiving battlefield upon which they meet, the evil that is the spawn of Sin and Death—given ruthless expression in the likes of Hitler's Final Solution, Eastern European and African Ethnic Cleansing, American chattel slavery and segregation, South African Apartheid, the economic and political imperialism of the Roman Pax Romana, in examples too legion to number—cannot be absolved, its ruin expiated. One does not atone for Sin and Death; one engages and obliterates them. Resurrection is God's silver bullet. When Jesus of Nazareth is raised from the depths of Hades, it is as though God, manipulating the dirt of the earth like the muzzle of a gun, shot him straight through the heart of an enemy otherwise impervious to every strategic and tactical maneuver against it. Then, and in the future to come, God triggers resurrection. It is resurrection that puts the enemy down. Resurrection's truth, resurrection's promise, and resurrection's historical reality must therefore be the primary proclamation of the apocalyptic preacher whom God deploys in God's formidable wake. That deployment makes the preacher God's weapon, too. For the resurrection warrior John of Patmos, the apocalyptic message that believers must affirm and preach in this combat context can be summed up in a simple phrase: Dawn of the Dead.

RESURRECTION AS AN APOCALYPTIC SYMBOL

Apocalyptic eschatology is fascinated with resurrection. The symbol that was most clearly expressed first in the book of Daniel took narrative flight in the imagery unleashed by later Jewish and Christian apocalyptic materials. Leander Keck observes: "And so there arose the view, first clearly expressed in the Book of Daniel, that at the end of history, God would intervene and vindicate the righteous who had paid with their lives for being obedient, and that God would do this by resurrecting them."[1] As Keck's observation suggests, this apocalyptic sensibility around resurrection implies a militaristic worldview: humans are caught up in a fight for their literal and metaphorical lives on a cosmic battleground.

Another essential characteristic of apocalyptic eschatology is eschatological dualism or, more colloquially put, the doctrine of the two ages. To use John of Patmos language, this present age is infested by the evil of a satanic red dragon and its two accomplice beasts (Rev. 12–13). So evil is this age, in fact, that it cannot be redeemed; it must be invaded, engaged, and reconfigured. Not destroyed. God, John declares, will make all things new (21:5), even the things of this evil age, apparently reclaiming them for their original purpose, setting an end to evil's dominance, but not bringing an end to the space-time reality in which evil once reigned. The dualism is therefore complex. Resident within the evil age is the promise of the past creation and the hope for a future reclamation. Between those two auspicious points, though, there is war. God will play God's part; humans must play their part. In fact, apocalyptic eschatology's sense of clarity, striking as it is, presumes to make it easier for humans to make a stand about where they belong. The eschatological dualism creates a moral dualism where right and wrong are as clearly differentiated as white and black. As the Christ-followers in Laodicea learned, there is no lukewarm gray, no neutral ground (Rev. 3:14–22). A side must be chosen. Radical choices must be made.[2]

Those choices are made on a cosmic landscape. Apocalyptic eschatology, though concerned about the individual, combats a preoccupation with individual piety through a much broader and more important focus. In their book on preaching apocalyptic texts, Paul Jones and Jerry Sumney put it well: "Stated crudely, apocalyptic texts are about God and community; they are not about me and you, God.'"[3] What J. Christiaan Beker notes in his discussion of apocalyptic eschatology in the writings of Paul is more than appropriate for John: "The human being is involved in the worldwide conflict between the kingdom of God and the kingdom of this world. In other words, for Paul there is no dualism between the human soul and the external world. He places the human being in the context of the world and its power structures."[4]

With God, then, humankind is caught up in a cosmic conflict whose ending will determine ownership of creation. Evil is real and it is universal and it has laid claim, in this age, to what was created by and rightfully belongs to God. God's sovereignty over God's world has been challenged. If God wants to protect and maintain that sovereignty, God must invade this age and reclaim it. Apocalyptic eschatology is determined that God will do just that. The future is so set, so designed, as to be ultimately, at least in this one respect, predictable. God will invade. God will win. "This belief reflects not a naive and romanticized notion that everything will work out for the best in the end, but an unshakable certainty that nothing can rival the ultimate sovereignty of God."[5]

The present, then, draws its true meaning and purpose not from the transitory circumstance of evil's having staked a claim over this age, but from the future certainty of God's imminent intervention. That intervention is more than a spiritual awakening; it is a social, historical, political, environmental, and indeed cosmic renewal and therefore liberation.[6] In God's sure, future act, this age and all those who have populated it will be transfigured and recovered. Evil's rule will become God's reign. God's people will be vindicated. That vindication will be expressed as bodily resurrection. Indeed, as Rev. 20:4–5 implies, a literal, bodily resurrection will be the tactical maneuver God deploys to bring that reign about.

One result of such a quick and admittedly oversimplified survey is an important moral and ethical observation. If, indeed, the responsive believer, pinned down on the cosmic battlefield, is called upon to act with God, choosing for God and against evil, what kind of action is required? More precisely to my own concern, if one of the principal tools of God's insurgency is the weapon of resurrection, is that a device that humans, hoping to respond to God by emulating God, can trigger? For me, that is a significant question for the person who would preach through the lens of New Testament apocalyptic eschatology.

The contemporary tendency, however, has been to give up the fight before it begins. Rather than get drawn into the apocalyptic worldview and the ethics it may or may not require, contemporary Christians, following a long line of established Christian theological and homiletical practice, dehistoricize apocalyptic materials with Albert Schweitzer and Karl Barth, demythologize them with Rudolf Bultmann into their supposed existential essence, or remythologize them into some more appropriate postmodern ethnic, gender, cultural, political, or liberationist derivation.[7]

The work of such seminal scholars presaged the decline of apocalyptic theology to come. American historian James Moorhead, appealing to the curious incident of the silent dog in the nighttime from Arthur Conan Doyle's stories of Sherlock Holmes, observes: "In mainstream Protestantism, apocalypticism was the dog that did not bark. Or to render the analogy more precise, it was the dog whose barking, muted from the outset, became ever fainter until it was little more than a whimper."[8] Moorhead's comment about *mainstream* Protestantism suggests a very important point. Apocalyptic thinking has been engaged, if in a wrongheaded way, by many contemporary sectarian movements. The Branch Davidians, who followed David Koresh's warped interpretation of the book of Revelation, are a key latter-day example.[9]

Given this "interesting" state of affairs, it is no wonder that Thomas Altizer can conclude: "The truth is that there is no mainstream Christian theologian in the twentieth century who is open to apocalypticism, or who has not wholly transformed it."[10] This academic avoidance provides an unfortunate pattern for preachers. Tom Long observes:

> Lectionary editors, for their part, cheerfully comply with the preacher's desire to avoid the more bizarre examples of apocalyptic texts. The Common Lectionary, for example, includes a few slices of apocalyptic material from the synoptics, but only three lessons from Daniel are listed, and the few lessons included from Revelation are all drawn from the relatively gentler hymnic sections of that book. One can travel blithely through the lectionary never opening any bottomless pit, never encountering sulphur belching from a mount, never seeing the moon drip blood, and never running into a beast making war on the saints.[11]

Even if one could convince Christians that apocalyptic eschatology has a pertinent preaching message for the mainstream church, one would still be hard pressed to develop a convincing argument that it has a pertinent message for the mainstream world. After all, an apocalyptic message, biblical or not, seems ill suited for a world that, as Beker puts it, continues stubbornly on.[12] Time does keep marching forward, and to make matters worse, aimlessly so. Or as Rennie Schoepflin puts it: "Time moved according to no inherent purpose and with no end in sight that might give ultimate meaning for the present."[13] And as Martin Marty observes, the movement of history, devoid of the truly miraculous in documentable time and circumstance, gives no indication of either God's present or planned involvement. "'God in history' is . . . a contradiction, a meaningless phrase. Wherever else God is, he is not in history, for if he were there would no longer be any history."[14]

None of this is good for resurrection. Resurrection language is trademark apocalyptic language; Jesus' resurrection from the dead is described in the Gospels and in Paul as a signature moment of God's direct intervention into this historical age, a moment that prefigures an even more invasive resurrection to take place in the imminent future.[15] If we cannot raise apocalyptic eschatology from the academic and homiletical dead, resurrection is bound to go down and stay down with it.

In this contemporary age, though, it is difficult to preach a literal resurrection of the dead—individual, mass, or otherwise—with a straight face. What is more scandalous than basing one's entire faith superstructure on a man who died with seditious criminals on a Roman cross? How about basing one's entire faith superstructure on the belief that this man literally got up from the dead, literally ascended into heaven, and is planning to return the same way he left, on the clouds, to raise everybody else from the dead? What is a rational believer supposed to do with all *that*? Dehistoricize it. Demythologize it. Remythologize it. At the very least, invite a guest pulpiteer to preach it.

One of the contemporary ironies of this mainstream Christian skittishness about apocalyptic resurrection eschatology is that humankind, in its secular guise, is caught up in one of the most apocalyptic periods in recent historical memory.[16] Lieven Boeve puts it well:

> We are confronted today with a remarkable paradox. . . . On the one hand, we live in a time in which apocalyptic ideas have virtually vanished from the Christian tradition, often on account of the dialogue between Christian faith and modernity: apocalypticism is too mythological, too dangerous, too literal, too speculative, too escapist. On the other hand, however, we are now faced with a "post-Christian" cultural environment in which apocalyptic is raising its head once again in the form of an "apocalyptic sentiment" which expresses itself, among other things, in a fear of the physical end of the world, of the moral collapse of the human race, and the ultimate meaninglessness of human existence and every human aspiration or thought.[17]

Boeve seems to be saying that in this resurgence of apocalyptic thinking, it is mainstream Christians who are being left behind. Driven by fears generated from two world wars, financial armageddons, threat of nuclear and now environmental and pandemic annihilation, the twentieth and twenty-first centuries have taken on an apocalyptic bearing in a secular guise.

Elizabeth Roesen introduces a compelling point:

> Here I am going to posit a convergence of historical events with eschatological implications, a growing climate of fear regarding them, and an equally powerful sense that the paradigms by which we have tried to understand and interpret our world have come to seem inadequate, and perhaps unusable. This nexus of social mood and historical condition creates a climate of anxious uncertainty that the traditional apocalyptic model is well structured to address.[18]

As Michael Barkun notes, these secular apocalyptic formulas are "in every way the functional equivalent of their religious predecessors, expressed in nonreligious idioms from which the supernatural has been purged."[19]

So enthralled by this secular apocalyptic sensibility is our contemporary world that the mainstream media has made a focused effort not only to pick up on the imagery, but also to warp it and capitalize from it. Stephen O'Leary chronicles four primary types of apocalyptic media that have surged in quantity and popular-culture relevance: monster movies, alien films, postapocalyptic films, and dramas of nuclear destruction.[20] He neglects to mention just as broad an array of written materials: novels, graphic novels, and nonfiction pieces whose story lines are driven by end-time, apocalyptic symbolism. It is through a sharper focus on the end that the authors of these pieces hope to clarify our understanding of the now.

In looking at the New Testament language of "resurrection" and "dead," I endeavor to follow their creative, cultural lead. But cautiously. To be sure, critics of apocalyptic eschatology have important and appropriate points to make. As Cook notes, the "blind spots" evident in an apocalyptic sensibility such as gender discrimination and ecological exploitation must neither be overlooked nor dismissed. They must be seriously engaged in a disciplined way through hermeneutical investigation. And yet, neither must the texts be domesticated.

Cook observes that the most common way of taming apocalyptic texts is the contemporary popular approach of treating them as coded documents. Once the code is broken, the key time lines related to key nations and individuals are revealed, so that the schedule for the imminent end can be mapped out and laid bare in the most predictable of ways. But there are also more sophisticated methods of domestication. Cook points to the work of Catherine Keller, who is so distraught by the problems of apocalyptic literature and theology that she seeks a counterapocalyptic movement. Keller, Cook helpfully notes, domesticates apocalyptic by exclusively using an anthropological lens to view this material, which intends to operate from a transcendent perspective. It is human purpose and expectation, not divine determination, that drives her reading of the material. And so she reads Revelation's passing away of heaven and earth (21:1) in favor of a new creation as a shocking indifference to the old creation. "A 'return to the '*nihilo*' is unacceptable to Keller, because it would spell 'an*nihil*ation.'"[21] Cook goes on to explain that Keller is right, from a human perspective. Apocalyptic eschatology, though, operates from a transcendent perspective. "In comparison to the heavenly, transcendent realm unveiled by the apocalyptic texts, the present world of human experience is fully incomplete and tenuous. It will do no good to treasure it as an eternal good. Making the survival of the present creation an unrestricted religious value, the apocalyptic literature claims, would be a case of idolatry."[22] Cook therefore concludes, "The harsh, offensive qualities of the literature call not for dismissal but for critical engagement and interpretive sophistication."[23]

For my purposes, this effort of critical engagement implies two key points. First, apocalyptic theology is mythic and symbolic. Even at the risk of being offensive, the apocalyptic author's intent is to deploy striking imagery that seduces or shocks the reader into an altered state of perceiving one's self and world, and God's movement in them both. When, for example, Will Willimon, rereads Christmas, as genial a season as exists, through an apocalyptic lens, he uncovers an unsettling symbolism of threat:

> Our real problem with these Advent/Christmas texts is largely political rather than merely intellectual. A great deal will depend on our social location. If you tell me, living in Durham [N.C.] with two healthy, well-fed, well-futured children, "This world is ending. [God is physically breaking into human history to liberate us from the oppressions of this world.] God has little vested interest in the present world order," I shall hear it as bad news.
>
> However, for a mother in a barrio in Mexico City who has lost four of her six children to starvation to hear, "This present world is not what God had in mind. God is not

> finished, indeed is now moving, to break down and to rebuild in Jesus," I presume that would sound something like gospel. For her, texts you will be asked to deliver this Advent/Christmas are not (as has been charged by some liberal critics) an invitation to "pie-in-the-sky, by-and-by" theology. They are a series of Molotov cocktails meant to ignite a revolutionary conflagration. They begin in the ghettos as whispered expectation among pushy slaves, as the clench-fisted yearning of displaced Hebrew refugees, as the cry of a baby born in a backstreet to an occupied people.[24]

Second, to engage apocalyptic symbolism in a way that hermeneutically connects its meaning and message to our world, the interpreter must be willing to suspend traditional norms of belief. Indeed, we do this all the time, and happily so, where more traditional biblical and theological imagery is concerned. David Jacobsen recognizes the regular occurrence of such suspension "when we allow the depth image of a symbol (say, a broken loaf) to call us, at least for a moment, out of our success anxieties to revel in the incalculable absurdities of grace."[25] However, the elitism of intellectual sophistication and logic will too often conclude that apocalyptic imagery is senseless, inappropriate, and meaningless. Even silly. Dismissing it and its contemporary, popular interpretative applications such as science fiction and horror films and writings renders us incapable of learning how to reread our world and time through any of these images and applications.

John's dramatization of combat with the forces of Satan on a cosmic battlefield was his attempt to shock his followers, who were accommodating themselves to Greek and Roman culture, with the realization that they were embroiled in a war whose reality and contours they did not understand. The disturbing imagery was meant to wake them up. Even if they did not fight in this war, or for that matter, even acknowledge that it was taking place, the war's outcome would determine their destiny.

Hermeneutically speaking, apocalyptic eschatology, through its unsettling symbolism, today maintains John's first-century aim: to wake hearers and readers to the devastating, devouring nature of their so-called "normal" existence. Which brings us to the dead. John makes sense of the normal world of the living by appealing to the abnormal symbolism of the dead.

THE DEAD ARE US

Resurrection starts with the Dead. As either thing, condition, or place, whether in the lofty, limited confines of academic discourse or in the base but much more fun and sometimes more illuminating expanses of popular culture, "dead" is not a static concept. It is instead a tensive symbol, pregnant with meaning potential that is contextually accessed and therefore contextually sharpened and often hardened into a particular meaning.[26]

Consider the contextual perspective of one Joe Ledger, a popular culture creation in the middling thriller novel *Patient Zero*. Part soldier, part detective, as an emissary of the alleged living, Joe engages an agent of the dead.

> Javad lunged forward again, his fingers tearing my shirt, his stink that of a carrion bird. No, . . . that wasn't right, that wasn't it. Javad's smell was that *of* carrion. He smelled like the dead. Because he *was* dead. This whole train of thought shot through my brain in a microsecond, its speed and clarity amplified by terror.[27]

Later, after surviving his odd encounter, Joe's terror is amplified even further when he learns that the dead man he encountered might be a harbinger of more dead men and women to come. In a conversation with a mysterious government supervisor whose outrageously unsubtle last name is Church, Joe demands and receives an answer he does not want to hear:

> "What was he?"
>
> We were back at the table. They'd let me clean up in a bathroom. I showered and dressed in borrowed gym clothes. The shakes had started in the shower. Adrenaline

> accounted for a lot of it, but it was more than that. After thirty minutes my hands were still trembling and I didn't care if Church saw it.
>
> [Church] shrugged. "We're still working on a name for his condition."
>
> "*Condition?* That son of a bitch was *dead*!"
>
> "From now on," Church said, "we may have to consider 'dead' a relative term."[28]

Contemporary secular-apocalyptic, popular novels and movies have an intriguing way of addressing the pregnant meaning potential of "dead": as a relative term whose meaning is capable of such imaginative and useful twisting.

Though allegedly alive, we, too, are preoccupied with death. Perhaps we are so capable in our popular culture of imagining the walking dead because there are times when we who ostensibly comprise the living seem so much like them. Consider this striking narration by Dr. Michihiko Hachiya, a Japanese physician writing in his classic *Hiroshima Diary* about his personal revelations following the nuclear devastation of his city:

> Those who were able walked silently toward the suburbs in the distant hills, their spirits broken, their initiative gone. When asked whence they had come, they pointed to the city and said "that way": and when asked where they were going, pointed away from the city and said "this way." They were so broken and confused that they moved and behaved like automatons.
>
> Their reactions had astonished outsiders who reported with amazement the spectacle of long files of people holding stolidly to a narrow rough path when close by was a smooth easy road going in the same direction. The outsiders could not grasp the fact that they were witnessing the exodus of a people who walked in the realm of dreams.[29]

The recounting of a Japanese grocer, himself severely burned, is even more arresting:

> The appearance of people was, . . . well, they all had skin blackened by burns. . . . They had no hair because their hair was burned, and at a glance you couldn't tell whether you were looking at them from in front or in back. . . . They held their arms bent [forward] like this [he proceeded to demonstrate their position], . . . and their skin—not only on their hands but on their faces and bodies too—hung down. . . . If there had been only one or two such people, perhaps I would not have had such a strong impression. But wherever I walked I met these people. . . . Many of them died along the road—I can still picture them in my mind—like walking ghosts. . . . They didn't look like people of this world. . . . They had a special way of walking—very slowly. . . . . I myself was one of them.[30]

Robert Jay Lifton, who compiles this and other dramatic Hiroshima accounts, wonders in the telling where the line that separates life from death resides. He opines: "These Hiroshima memories, then, combine explicit end-of-the-world imagery with a grotesque dreamlike aura of nonnatural situation, a form of existence in which life was so permeated by death as to become virtually indistinguishable from it."[31]

I am interested in this *relativity* of "dead" because John of Patmos was also so interested. In his book, John reconfigures "dead" by cloaking it in the accoutrements of life. By the time he is finished, the dead and the living share so many traits that it is almost impossible to tell them apart:

> When he opened the fifth seal, I saw under the altar the souls of those who had been slaughtered for the word of God and for the testimony they had given; they cried out with a loud voice, "Sovereign Lord, holy and true, how long will it be before you judge and avenge our blood on the inhabitants of the earth?" They were each given a white robe and told to rest a little longer, until the number would be complete both of their fellow servants and of their brothers and sisters, who were soon to be killed as they themselves had been killed. (Rev. 6:9–11)

Are these killed souls dead or alive? If they are dead, why are they so animated? If they are alive, how is it that they have been killed?

In chapter 7 the potential for meaning is equally expansive, not to mention confusing:

> After this I looked [into heaven], and there was a great multitude that no one could count, from every nation, from all tribes and peoples and languages, standing before the throne and before the Lamb, robed in white, with palm branches in their hands. (Rev. 7:9)

> Then one of the elders addressed me, saying, "Who are these, robed in white, and where have they come from?" I said to him, "Sir, you are the one that knows." Then he said to me, "These are they who have come out of the great ordeal; they have washed their robes and made them white in the blood of the Lamb. For this reason they are before the throne of God, and worship him day and night within his temple, and the one who is seated on the throne will shelter them. They will hunger no more, and thirst no more; the sun will not strike them, nor any scorching heat; for the Lamb at the center of the throne will be their shepherd, and he will guide them to springs of the water of life, and God will wipe away every tear from their eyes." (Rev. 7:13–17)

They died. In the great ordeal. And yet, they do not seem dead at all. They live. And yet they do not live as we live. They live somehow better. Because they are dead!

In chapter 20, John directly connects this dying and living, living and dying, to the concept of resurrection:

> Then I saw thrones, and those seated on them were given authority to judge. I also saw the souls of those who had been beheaded for their testimony to Jesus and for the word of God. They had not worshiped the beast or its image and had not received its mark on their foreheads or their hands. They came to life and reigned with Christ a thousand years. (The rest of the dead did not come to life until the thousand years were ended.) This is the first resurrection. (Rev. 20:4–5)

Beheaded. One does not get much more dead than that. Executed by a satanically inspired imperial Beast and its local proxy governments, the human and institutional representations of Death and Hades on earth. And yet these beheaded folks live and reign with Christ, not in heaven this time, but on earth. Right here. The living, presumably walking, definitely ruling *dead*. They take over the earth. As a part of God's first resurrection. A first resurrection that is the prelude to a massive, universal, literal dawn to life for all the dead.

What are these living dead? And perhaps more important, what do they see when they look at us?

I have spent most of my academic career focused on cultural interpretation, reading and understanding the text through the lens of particular cultures, especially my own African American culture. I do this because I work from the premise that language is a cultural phenomenon constructed and then deconstructed, decoded, and subsequently interpreted contextually. The words, sentences, and paragraphs that comprise narrative texts do not contain meaning, but have meaning potential. That potential is culturally appropriated. It is therefore not odd to me that people from different cultural locations can read the same biblical text and derive a different meaning from it. I understand that they may well have accessed different segments of the text's overall meaning potential. The difficulty arises, of course, when a cultural reader demands that one's own *particular* access of the meaning potential is all the meaning the text has to offer.

This fascination with the cultural location of an interpreter and the impact that location has on the meaning an interpreter derives from a text or circumstance drives me to a perhaps morbid but certainly fascinating question: What "meaning" does an executed soul *living* either in heaven (now) or on earth (following what John calls the first resurrection of the dead) attribute to the meaning potentiality of the term "living," a term that we who occupy this historical age religiously claim for ourselves?

In this historical age, our reality and our truth are bound up in the myth of our "aliveness." We *are* alive! But if the souls in heaven that John chronicles in chapters 6 (vv. 9–11), 7 (vv. 9–17), and 20 (vv. 4–5) are "alive," then, since we are distinct from them, we must be, by definition, something else. At least, we are something else according to John's apocalyptic viewpoint that reveals the truth about "life." Life is direct proximity to God in the heavenly throne room (6:9–11; 7:9; 20:4) and ultimately direct proximity to God on earth (21:3). The preunderstanding that derives from this direct life relation with God is described in 7:16 as existence without sadness or mourning and then later at 21:4 as devoid even of Death. This, for John, is what "life" looks like.

What, then, are we? Some degree of dead. Distant from God. In direct proximity to the animate power that John calls Death and Hades (1:18; 6:8; 20:13–14; 21:4), living itself out through the satanic possession of the Beasts from the sea and land. Lifton's observation about the Japanese memories in the aftermath of the Hiroshima bomb describes the condition of our entire historical age with equal precision: "a form of existence in which life [is] so permeated by death as to become virtually indistinguishable from it."[32]

Living Dead. Walking Dead. It is, of course, the pop culture image of the zombie. The zombie has become so ingrained in secular apocalyptic popular culture, so potent a science-fictional theme, that even the most highly regarded of contemporary scientific institutions have taken notice of it. Thus a May 19, 2011, article by CNN can report: "The Centers for Disease Control and Prevention is a big, serious government agency with a big, serious job: protecting public health from threats ranging from hurricanes to bird flu. So when the good doctors of Atlanta warned people this week about how to prepare for a zombie apocalypse, the world took notice."[33]

In his book *Gospel of the Living Dead*, Kim Paffenroth sees secular apocalyptic symbolism at play:

> More than any other monster, zombies are fully and literally apocalyptic, as the movies acknowledge (especially *Dawn of the Dead* [2004]): they signal the end of the world

> as we have known it for thousands of years. . . . Also, in the original meaning of "apocalyptic," they "reveal" terrible truths about human nature, existence, and sin.[34]

As in the book of Revelation (cf. 14:20; 17:16; 19:18), these zombie tales "contain scenes of graphic, usually unspeakable violence, often including the most sickening acts of cannibalism and dismemberment, depicted in excruciating detail with rivers and geysers of blood."[35] These stories shock us with their portrayal of the depths of depravity to which we humans are capable of descending. And yet, in some more firm ways, using and even delighting in the strangest forms of humor, the symbolism is meant to share not only what humans are capable of, but also what humans have already become. For example, the portrayed cannibalism is a wicked play on the human tendency to consume each other and the environmental space we inhabit.[36]

In this grotesque world, humans and monsters often become hard to distinguish, "and therefore the moral rules that guide our dealings with humans—it is better to suffer injustice than to commit it, thou shalt not kill, love thy neighbor, turn the other cheek—are discarded as irrelevant and unfeasible."[37] Indeed, there are moments when the humans seem less human than the walking dead they struggle to overcome. "The zombies' victory is facilitated in all the movies by the humans' constant inability to cooperate with one another, an inability frequently exacerbated by racism, while the zombies themselves, though usually oblivious to one another, are always a multi-ethnic mob whose violence is always directed outwards."[38] It is tongue-in-cheek social criticism that strikes a devastating blow at the pride that humans are creation's exceptional creatures.

> It is the most extreme and funniest reversal that the world once dominated by humans—who so arrogantly and stupidly suppose that they are the smartest, most advanced, and most important life forms in the universe—is destroyed pretty easily by an apocalyptic army, not of powerful supernatural beings, like Satan or the Antichrist, but of slow, clumsy imbeciles who can barely stand up. The whole

> idea of zombies taking over the world is both a funny and potent parable against human hubris, arrogance, and self-sufficiency.[39]

Zombies are a metaphor for conflict and catastrophe. In a literal sense, there has been some devastation, biological, nuclear, or so forth. In a figurative sense, the reader/viewer is compelled to compare the walking-dead reality to one's own natural reality and thereby realize what John was trying to get his readers to understand: what we call "normal" life is itself a crisis situation. We simply do not see it yet. To make the point more fine: we are not waiting for the walking dead; we already *are* the walking dead. We will not one day be running from zombies; we are, via the angle of the contextual lens used by the souls in heaven, already zombies. This is the normal "crisis" we live with every day, have lived with every day since Adam's unfortunate infelicity in the garden. Contemporary apocalyptic hermeneutics needs recognition of no other crisis event or moment. It needs nothing other than our "normal" symbolic existence as the living dead.

Perhaps, in the end, this is helpful symbolism for persons preaching to a faltering American church, becoming smaller and less powerful by the day, on a cultural island as the secular world takes over, as more and more its adherents become the outsiders and the outcast, the remnant struggling against the overwhelming tide. What is it that the church should seek and the preacher should preach? Life? In the heavenly realm, to be sure. But what about here? What is possible here in a world that by definition is separate from God, a world occupied by those of us who, within the church and without, are by definition, then, the animate dead? What should we preach to this world? Resurrection! But to understand the apocalyptic significance of resurrection, we must first appreciate the meaning of death.

We begin by preaching the truth that the symbolism of the Apocalypse conveys. Dead is a relative term. So is life. One cannot comprehend the truth of the one without counterposing it against the other. I would make the case that John understands four levels of creaturely human existence: *life*, *dead (type A)*, *dead dead (type B)*, and *living dead.*

Earlier we have described *life* by way of allusion to texts like Revelation 6:9–11; 7:9–17; and 20:4–5. Life is existence in direct proximity to God. At 2:10, the child of humanity voices a paradox: "Be faithful until death, and I will give you the crown of life." This is that ethic of life imaged in the heavenly throne room. Those who are faithful in the witness to the lordship of Jesus Christ, though they are killed for that stubbornness, shall be rewarded with something they have heretofore not possessed: *life*. Indeed, in all of the letters to the seven churches (Rev. 2–3), John concludes with a comparable promise about the reward of "life," which is, by definition, that time and space when the believer is in proximate relationship with God for all time.[40]

Life is easy. Death is mesmerizing in its complexity. There is first what I would call a *type A death*, or more colloquially put, "dead." To be dead is to have one's earthly existence terminated. This is the kind of death John alludes to at 9:6: "People will seek death." It is the type of death associated with the preliminary acts of judgment that follow the opening of the first six seals, the sounding of the first six trumpets, and the pouring out of the first six bowls. It is type A death to which John refers at 2:23, when the child of humanity warns that he will strike the children of Jezebel dead. It is type A death that the fourth apocalyptic horseman brings at 6:8. Babylon's death at 18:8 is type A death. Type A death brings a merciful end to the preliminary judgment acts of God.

But if type A death is meted out as a punishment for those who resist God and persecute Christ's witnesses, it also is used against Christ's witnesses as a means of stamping that witness out. Antipas, an exemplar witness, suffers type A death at 2:13. And 6:11 promises that many witnesses will soon suffer type A death. The two prototypical and metaphorical witnesses suffer type A death at 11:7. Clearly, the beheaded witnesses of 20:4–5 have suffered a similar fate. Type A death does not discriminate. Sooner or later, it comes to believer and nonbeliever alike.

Being dead, though, is a fate better than death itself. John's hearers and readers know that being type A dead is not final because there are multiple occasions in the narrative where the seer confirms that life exists beyond it. Even the mortally wounded beast can be resurrected beyond type A death (13:3, 12). At 20:13, those captured by death rise to new life.[41] One of the benefits for those who enjoy life will be the complete cessation of type A death (21:4).

Beyond being type A dead, though, there is dead dead. We will call it *type B death* (20:6, 14; 21:8). According to 2:11, those who have been faithful witnesses in their first life will not endure a second death. This second, type B death is for John a permanent cessation of existence. It is the death that follows a guilty verdict at the final judgment. Type B death, then, is the death one should fear. Revelation 20:13 indicates that at God's final judgment a decision will be made as to whether those who have died type A death will be accorded life or type B death. God makes this ruling on the basis of how a person has lived in historical existence.[42]

While type B death is to be avoided at all costs, there are circumstances where type A death is preferable even to historical existence. This historical existence, in other words, is so problematic that it is not the reward one seeks, but the destiny one ultimately hopes to overcome. The bleakest of historical circumstances involve humans like those of 9:6, who seek type A death as an escape from the torture of the demon locusts. They surely do not long for type B death, a permanent cessation, but for a release from this historical age and the struggles it represents. Even believers, witnesses to the lordship of Christ, may and often do prefer type A death to the persecution that comes from living out their faithful testimony. Indeed, it is by acting out their faith in such a relentless way that they not only may meet type A death, but may also conquer the evil satanic presence that wields it (12:10–11). This death is so transitory that it is not to be feared.

In John's apocalyptic imagination, death is clearly not a static concept. It is a fluid symbolic reality that allows for movement. It is relative. One enters it, and one moves beyond it, to a second, more final form of death, . . . or to life. That life is presently with God in the heavenly realm, as 6:9–11 and 7:9–17 demonstrate, or anticipated with Christ during his earthly reign (20:4–5), or on the reconfigured earth, symbolized as the new Jerusalem (Rev. 21–22). But life does not exist in this historical age. What we have here in this historical age is something else, something that is an antitype of the no mourning, no dying, and no darkness that typifies the new heaven and new earth. What we have here is something that mimics living but is akin to being dead. It is an age ruled by a satanic dragon and the beasts operating at its behest (Rev. 12–13). It is existence under constant pressure and duress, especially for those who would witness against the lordship of the dragon and its beasts. In its purest apocalyptic sense, it is an evil age. An age typified by the characteristics of death. Those of us who exist here, though not type A dead, and surely not type B dead, are also not alive, though we do oddly mimic the living who look down upon us with both horror and empathy from the heavenly throne room (6:9–11). Here we are consumed by the satanic dragon and its imperial forces that rule this age. In imitative response, we consume one another and the environment we inhabit. It is no wonder that the symbolic language best fitting our circumstance is "living dead."

RESURRECTION AS INVASION

For God to save us, God must invade. God's primary weapon is resurrection. The Lamb's resurrection. And then ours. In her wonderful essay on whether apocalyptic can be relevant to our time, Sophie Laws conjectures that in the book of Revelation "the apocalyptic perspective is altered in light of the cross."[43] It is a potent statement, belying the fact that the word "cross" never appears in the apocalypse, and the single reference to the verb "crucify" at 11:8 is more a historical reference than a theological starting point. To be sure, at 1:5, John does mention that Jesus redeemed humankind from their sins by his blood. Curiously, though, if this is a point that he wants to develop as fully as say the apostle Paul, why does he never mention the point again? In fact, one might argue that even at 1:5, John's central focus is not on Christ's death as much as it is on his identity as the faithful witness who is firstborn of the dead, the first resurrected one. This witness, made to suffer death because of that witness, comes back from the dead to witness in resurrected life. It is as though this resurrection makes the point that his witness and the claim to lordship it represents is true, despite—not because of, but despite—the fact of his slaughter. At 1:18, Christ himself proclaims that now, as the resurrected one, he lives. His life now is distinct from what it was before. He was dead, but now he lives. And that invasive resurrection came with a spoil of war: the keys to Death and Hades. Christ has the keys and can and will therefore unlock the doors of Death and Hades and liberate all who have been consigned to their type A death by the satanic dragon and its imperial beasts. This is the "saving" resurrection message that John repeats over and over throughout his Apocalypse. Christ does not save because he died; Christ saves because, resurrected, he lives. And in living, he holds the keys that unlock Death.

In chapter 5, to be sure, the Lamb is worthy because he was slaughtered. But is that the worthiness of an atoning lamb slaughter? The work of Loren Johns is particularly helpful here. Looking at the rhetorical force of the Lamb symbolism in the Apocalypse, Johns, after surveying the lamb imagery in early Judaism, concludes that "there is no evidence at this point to establish the existence of anything like a recognizable redeemer-lamb figure in [its] apocalyptic traditions."[44] John would therefore not have expected his readers to connect the lamb's suffering/slaughter to their own redemption. In fact, after a survey of the Hebrew Bible, Johns concludes that "the terminology used in the Apocalypse does not fit well with the lambs of the sacrificial system."[45] In fact, John does not restrict slaughter language to the Lamb (see 6:4, 9; 13:3; 18:24). Johns thus argues that slaughter language of the Lamb at 5:6 is not primarily expiatory. In fact, he argues that "there is little in the Apocalypse of John to support this understanding of Jesus' death as Atonement."[46]

Indeed, it is also difficult to imagine what kind of atonement could possibly assuage Death. Death clearly has a voracious appetite; it is hard to imagine a single killing of any kind satisfying it. Why would Death accept even the highest profile killing or a massive amount of killing as payment for a future existence freed from death? For Death to operate so would be for Death to operate against its own expansive interests. Even Death must know that a kingdom so divided against itself will not long stand (Mark 3:23–27).

In John's narrative context, the Lamb is worthy because he did what all the believers are expected to do (12:11): he witnessed even when faced with death. His worthiness resides in his witnessing; his witnessing is the effort John's followers, like John himself, are called to emulate.

In the broader thematic and apocalyptic context, where this age is in the grips of the powers that wield death, and by all accounts humans are the living dead—dying, even on a cross, neither gets one noticed nor dramatically alters the situation on the ground. The dead simply do not notice other dead. And the purveyors of death rejoice whenever death occurs to whomever it occurs because they have one more entity to lock away in Hades. Adding to the dead is not a drawback for those committed to making the relativity of death a static reality forever in Hades. In a world typified by death, killings, even high-profile killings, do not raise a transforming alarm. In a world typified by death, what brings notice that something transformative is on the horizon is life in the face of death, life even after death, life in spite of death, life that unlocks the doors and thus breaks the power of death. What the purveyors of death notice is defiant life. It is resurrection that frightens them. As Martinus de Boer recognizes, Christian thinking modifies Jewish apocalyptic at just this point: ". . . the hour of the eschaton was not, as in Jewish apocalyptic eschatology, about to strike; it had already struck in God's raising of Jesus from the dead, an apocalyptic-eschatological event."[47] The dramatic turn of the ages, from an age captive to satanic power, to an age where satanic power has been overturned, occurs with the Lamb's rise from the dead (12:5). Jesus' resurrection, then, is God's ultimate weapon.

When John repeatedly warns, at the opening and close of his work, that this resurrected Christ is coming soon (2:16; 3:11; 22:7, 12, 20), he is sounding the alarm for a grand, sweeping, universal invasion. By engaging the trigger of Christ's resurrected return, God will detonate the Dawn of all the Dead to life. Their liberation, their "aliveness" will concretize the truth of God's complete and total cosmic dominance (20:13–14). The dead will rise up and invade our space, the space of this historical era, the space of the living dead, overwhelming it and transforming it into a realm of life. Only life can conquer death. In this final resurrection, God will have made that point perfectly clear.

PREACHING THE DAWN OF THE DEAD

Our homiletical task is to anticipate the reality and effect of God's resurrection point in our contemporary resurrection preaching. Surely this is what John means when he says, "They have conquered him through the blood of the Lamb and through the word of their testimony" (12:11). Through their testimony, they participated in God's conquest of the powers that haunt this age. Through their testimony to resurrection life, with God, they have conquered death! Their testimony was to the lordship of the resurrected Lamb, whose own resurrection was a harbinger of theirs to come. For John, to preach the truth and power of that resurrection is to conquer; for John, to preach the truth and power of that resurrection is to give God's end-time invasion a potent real-time effect (cf. 19:7–8).

Our homiletical task, then, is to overcome our modern and postmodern skittishness and proclaim the contemporary relevance of this imminent Dawn of the Dead through the "revealing" lens of both religious and secular apocalyptic eschatology. We begin by preaching in ways that challenge our current worldview, in ways that force us to see that we humans are not in charge of the world we call our own, that we are in the midst of a crisis we do not fully comprehend. Arrogantly convinced that we live, we do not fully appreciate the consequence of having been captured by death, walking unwittingly under its control. Preaching apocalyptic eschatology in this circumstance is not, as Boeve helpfully puts it, "simply a matter of devastation, catastrophe and chaos, it is also one of perspective, revelation and disclosure."[48] And that is why contemporary Christian apocalyptic preaching "calls for a shift from catastrophe thinking to crisis thinking."[49] The crisis is prompted by the truth of our condition, the truth that apocalyptic preachers must be committed to proclaiming: we *are* the living dead. Thus we face pertinent questions: How do we crisis preach to congregations of living dead who are committed to the conceit that they are alive? What will such preaching do and mean for the way we walking dead Christians engage our work and our world?

The first thing I think preachers do is embrace the secular apocalyptic imagery streaming in at us from popular culture. Embrace it and reconfigure it so that it becomes capable of carrying the New Testament apocalyptic message. Already, secular apocalyptic imagery targets Christian perspectives, attacking and disrupting while we go blithely on our pious way. The longer we stand by and watch, creatively helpless, the more like a vacant, desolate zombieland our faith tradition becomes. In its zombie imagery, contemporary culture is laughing at biblical apocalyptic eschatology and its core weapon of resurrection, and many Christians do not seem to get the joke. Worse, many Christians do not seem even to realize that there is a joke.

The idea of the walking dead, the zombie, is a secular caricature of apocalyptic resurrection symbolism that has no creative response from the Christian homiletical side. The secular imagery promotes a world-ending catastrophe that yet allows us to live on, as if alive, though dead. A mock general and invasive resurrection. Those who escape the initial holocaust are hunted down by the imperialism of the walking dead, who seek out all who are not their kind, consuming some, infecting others, evangelizing in their own way until the world itself becomes all their own. This is an apocalyptic invasion of sorts, but it is an invasion aimed at taking life rather than giving it. It is the same image that John intends in the general resurrection of the dead who approach the new Jerusalem. They, too, are an army. They, too, capture and control. But they capture death and install life. How will they do it? Impossible in this historical era to say since we do not have the explanatory constructs. Perhaps, to borrow from contemporary secular apocalyptic imagery, it will be a polar opposite zombie phenomenon: the resurrected living, fanning out in indefatigable waves, consuming the living dead, infecting the living dead with the virus of resurrection life, and in the process transfiguring them.

Yes, it is silly. But this is the true *apocalyptic* stumbling block and folly of our faith, not a crucified leader. There are martyrs aplenty. But there was only one raised from the dead to reign at the right hand of God who is also the firstborn of all the dead who will imminently be raised. That is the true lunacy. But that is also the heart of the apocalyptic gospel and the place where the apocalyptic preacher must begin. Not on the cross. But with the raising of the dead. The raising of the one. The raising of the many. The Dawn of the Dead. That is the symbolism of resurrection as a weapon aimed at engaging, transfiguring, and then reclaiming this death-dealing historical age that is infested by the walking, living dead.

This proclamation must be anything but lukewarm. Having made the hearer cognizant about the truth of this world, the apocalyptic preacher makes a purposeful and somewhat controversial choice. As Jones and Sumney declare, "*The apocalyptic preacher forces a collision between the world that is and a world she or he imagines or anticipates.*"[50] And then the preacher forces the hearer to decide: exist in the world of the living dead, *or* enlist as a fighting member of the advance forces who prepare for the resurrection dawn. Beker makes the point well: "God's act in Christ focuses our attention on the present time as an 'apocalyptic' time, that is, on the either-or of our allegiance: do we *either* serve Christ *or* [serve] the powers of this world?"[51] Sophie Laws understands that this kind of apocalyptic theological commitment "may provide support for a real theology of liberation, rather than of a development or evolution, and for a hope of freedom expanded to a cosmic dimension."[52] I am reminded of Martin Luther King Jr.'s explanation of why African Americans could not wait for freedom and civil rights to evolve in his *Letter from a Birmingham Jail.* The time for lukewarm waffling was done. A definitive stand had to be taken. Either one was operating for life *or* committed to the forces of living death. There was, in such a case, no true middle ground. There never is when the opposing realities are death, even living death, and life. The apocalyptic preacher, standing from a perch where he can see the resurrection dawn, is committed to preaching and inciting life.

What does this mean concretely? It means focusing on the invasion symbolism, but focusing on God's invasive maneuver as the insurgency of life rather than death. Martyrdom, suffering, and dying—these are the not the transfiguring goal of God's invasive strategy so conceived. The primary ethic in John's Apocalypse is that believers should witness for the lordship of the resurrected Lamb, not that they should die for that lordship message. John was no less a witness because he did not lose his life but instead was exiled. Yes, in certain circumstances such witnessing may well cost a believer's life, and every believer should be willing to pay that price, seeing that the type A death imposed is a relative condition and not an enduring state. And yet the goal of witnessing is not death but the proclamation of the new life initiated by God's resurrection of the Lamb and God's impending resurrection of all the dead.

And that means, in the end, preaching the resurrection as fervently and more often than preaching the cross. Preaching resurrection is not just for Easter anymore. We must find a way to image it, to affirm our expectation for it, and to find ways to recast it in contemporary symbolism that connects with our contemporary age. But how can we do it? How would we symbolize ourselves to the world if the symbol were not a cross, an image of death to which the living dead can certainly relate, but the Dawn of Life. For John, it was the new Jerusalem, a hopeful image that still had cachet in a world where the real Jerusalem and its magnificent temple had existed only two decades earlier. What about the twenty-first century, when Jerusalem is a contested historical site that images more of the living dying that we are trying to overcome than the resurrected possibility to which we aspire? Can we image resurrection? Can we give sharp focus to God's Dawn of the Dead in a positively meaningful and serious way?

I argue that the very attempt would immobilize us. And perhaps that is a good thing, because we will not be able to do with God's ultimate invasive strategy what we have done with the cross. I have noticed how Christians chafe at branding language, as if that is a commercial, secular perversion that we folks of faith avoid. And yet, in the way we treat it, the Nike Swoosh has nothing on the Christian cross. We have branded ourselves with the cross in a way that is almost impossible where resurrection is concerned. We cannot hang resurrection around our necks, stick resurrection on our walls, hold resurrection up before our causes. We cannot domesticate it, control it, contain it. And perhaps that is exactly how it should be. Because in that moment of inability we are faced with the realization that we are a part of something much larger than ourselves, something we cannot form, hold, or manipulate.

And yet, as apocalyptic preachers, we are called, I believe, to incite our listeners to conjure the symbolism of resurrection in the way John so successfully crafts the powerful image of the new Jerusalem at the close of his work. It is not an image one can control. Who can control the idea of a city descending from heaven? But it is an image that invites participation. How do I become a citizen of it? The very question compels creative action. How do I help build it? It ought to be difficult to sing the poetic song of the new Jerusalem without wanting to help build it, find citizenship within it. No matter the cost.

That may well be John's point. John was preaching to a church struggling to survive, struggling, by all accounts, against the very trajectory of history: the imperial power, economic force, civil and pagan religions, and future of Rome. John's instruction was that his anti-Roman believers should engage history's trajectory and Rome's future by standing up and witnessing to an anti-Roman truth that would force Rome's representatives to engage, punish, and perhaps even destroy them. The seven churches were a community of believers facing figurative and literal death. John pressed them to stand in the face of that death and jeer it by declaring loud and missionary allegiance to the very anti-Roman claim the powers desired to stamp out: the resurrection and lordship of Jesus Christ. John counseled them to accept the challenge of living Christ's resurrection with the promise that as they preached it, so would they participate in it—as citizens of the new Jerusalem, in the here and now. The dead and their vision would rise. They participated now in that future Dawn by witnessing to the very resurrection life that made the powers want to destroy them.

In my own family history and individual research, I have used the imagery of African American slaves and the Civil Rights movement as illustrative examples. They are important to me because they represent the living dead, humans owned by other humans, humans declared by constitutional mandate to be only three-fifths of other humans, humans segregated and cordoned off from polite society because they were regarded as subhuman in some important ways. These people envisioned and embodied resurrection. And they used it as a weapon. They preached exodus when they were in Egypt. They drew education down from the sky when there was no legal opportunity for it on this earth. They faced down dogs, police, water cannons, and entire regions of hostility when there seemed to be no way safe way forward. Because they glimpsed what resurrection beyond slavery looked like, what resurrection beyond segregation looked like, and then embodied it and preached it, even though the very living of it brought more of the living-death force of slavery and segregation down upon their heads.

They lived resurrection until they participated in the unleashing of resurrection. They used resurrection as a weapon.

In this world preoccupied by and identified with death, the idiom of death no longer stands out on the human horizon. It no longer captures the spiritual imagination. It is no longer a stumbling folly or intellectual foolishness to believe that a messiah can be killed. Across the last twenty centuries, we have managed to kill bushels of messiahs, messianic movements, and messianic ideals. We know death. We are death. What we do not get, what strikes us as unfathomable, as foolishly beyond our reach, is life. Bleeding out here in the present, we do not get what it means to live renewed by the future. We certainly do not get what it means, having envisioned that future, to bring it to life in the here and now. Resurrection stands out in this world because resurrection is not normal: it makes no true sense in this world.

How do we find a way, like the African American slaves and the civil rights protestors who were their offspring, to mimic prophetic, invasive behavior in our everyday encounters of social, political, economic, and ecclesial life? How do we envision the invasive movement of outrageous new life into the midst of normal dying and then realize that vision in our preaching and our living, the way God realized Jesus' rising from the dead and now intends to realize our own? Our preaching task is to help our communities of the living and faithful dead figure out how to make such an envisioned force-of-life invasion come about. Our task is to make the descriptive mantra of the little boy in the movie *The Sixth Sense* become a prescriptive agenda for the community of faith. Our preaching task is to make the entire world *see* dead people—and not just see us all for what we are, the living dead, but also to commission our communities of living dead to engage a visible agenda of resurrection as participants in the cosmic war that God has already engaged.

In the summer of 2011, I had the good fortune to journey with some friends to Turkey and Patmos to visit the archaeological sites where the people who populated John's churches once lived. I thought of John's people as the remains of the great temples of Greco-Roman lordship loomed across the horizons, vast and mighty beyond all compare. And I thought of John's little house churches and the people huddling within, wondering how they were to compete with all of that. And I heard John telling them to use Jesus' resurrection as their weapon. To see the future of Jesus' lordship and live it until the reality of the world became it. A new and different Jerusalem.

A friend on our journey told me that he heard that message. And that it frightened him. He wanted me to help him do something with either the message or the fear. The message of John to witness to resurrected life in the midst of death is frightening because who can live like that all the time? You see injustice, and you want to speak for justice. You see impoverishment, and you want to speak for a sharing of resources, mine and yours. You see entire waves of people destroyed by prejudices and oppression, and you know that to live resurrection, to see and enact equality and liberation, is to be drawn into a fight you are not sure you can win. But you do know that the cost will be high. And yet we have our own lives to live, the futures of our own families to protect. How can we tend to both simultaneously? We cannot. But how can we then live with ourselves? I do not know what to tell that friend about living with both the desire to live resurrection and the simultaneous fear that to do so may bring figurative and perhaps literal death instead. I do not know what to tell a person what might happen after they fire a weapon; I only know to keep telling them that, in war, they are called to fire it. To fire resurrection into the midst of living death. No matter the cost. A radical, apocalyptic choice.

One final popular culture reference. Also in the summer of 2011, I read an appealing, inviting review about the novel *The Last Werewolf.* The novel is violent. It is sexual. It is faithless. It is distressing. It is also very funny, incredibly irreverent, and very well written. But all of that is beside the point. The novel is hard to read because it narrates the life of a man who is the very epitome of living death. He has lived for centuries in a cursed state of virtual death, unleashed on the full moon, to draw death down upon others. The curse makes him a missionary of death.

It is odd to be drawn inside the mind of a monster who knows that he is a monster but knows he cannot do other than monstrous things because of the curse that possesses him. It is odd to feel sympathy for a monster. It is creepy to wonder whether a monster resides inside me, too. There must have been fifteen times that I put that novel down and said, "I can't read this thing anymore." And fifteen times I picked it back up because I had to know what happens next for this man who brings death to life. And then there was a moment, after I had turned the last page, when it dawned on me that the reason I do not have an answer for my friend is that there are no answers, at least in this lifetime, for a curse. And we are living dead under the spell of a curse. John, bound on Patmos, drawn up to the heavens after he had been thrown to the earth, cannot escape the visions, as horrible as they are, and cannot let his people escape them either. Cursed. Those slaves and those marchers, seeing mountaintops while they were being destroyed in the valleys of life, could not escape the visions of the future, and they could not let their people escape them either. Cursed. Cursed with the vision of the future in the midst of the present. It is the curse of resurrection life that infects us living dead. The curse of a resurrected Lord who promises resurrection to us all. Like the voracious fever that relentlessly returns and drives a lion into a pack of wildebeest, the dizzying, insane pull of resurrection, the madness to resurrect justice and wholeness and circumstances and people writhes within us and resists our damnable determination to just keep blending into our historical era's massive company of the walking, living dead.

Like John, we are cursed with the task of finding and proclaiming a contemporary, poetic symbol that sings this song of resurrection and uncovers the truth about our age—that we are the living dead—and reveals the truth about God's past and planned invasion in a way that summons the living dead to enlist in God's war effort. Some image like . . . the Dawn of the Dead.

Chapter 2
Call of Duty
A Sermon

Preached on the occasion of a special Presbytery (of the James) worship service commemorating the 200th year of Union Presbyterian Seminary. The service was held at the Greater Richmond Convention Center on April 22, 2012.

THE EPIC STRUGGLE OF REVELATION 12

A great portent appeared in heaven: a woman clothed with the sun, with the moon under her feet, and on her head a crown of twelve stars. She was pregnant and was crying out in birth pangs, in the agony of giving birth. Then another portent appeared in heaven: a great red dragon, with seven heads and ten horns, and seven diadems on his heads. His tail swept down a third of the stars of heaven and threw them to the earth. Then the dragon stood before the woman who was about to bear a child, so that he might devour her child as soon as it was born. And she gave birth to a son, a male child, who is to rule all the nations with a rod of iron. But her child was snatched away and taken to God and to his throne; and the woman fled into the wilderness, where she has a place prepared by God, so that there she can be nourished for one thousand two hundred sixty days. And war broke out in heaven; Michael and his angels fought against the dragon. The dragon and his angels fought back, but they were defeated, and there was no longer any place for them

> in heaven. The great dragon was thrown down, that ancient serpent, who is called the Devil and Satan, the deceiver of the whole world—he was thrown down to the earth, and his angels were thrown down with him. Then I heard a loud voice in heaven, proclaiming, "Now have come the salvation and the power and the kingdom of our God and the authority of his Messiah, for the accuser of our comrades has been thrown down, who accuses them day and night before our God. But they have conquered him by the blood of the Lamb and by the word of their testimony, for they did not cling to life even in the face of death." (Rev. 12:1–11)

Do you know what a bucket list is? Do you have a bucket list? I have one. And the bucket I carry it in is real heavy, because the list is soooo long. And my list is so long it takes a real big bucket to contain it. I am convinced that I have a whole lot of time, so I have filled up my bucket with a whole lot of *stuff* I am hoping to do before God calls me up to that great big seminary in the sky. If I don't get to put a check mark beside a healthy number of things on my bucket list before my name is announced in the presbytery meeting roll call up yonder, I am prepared to throw an eschatological temper tantrum on those heavenly streets paved with gold.

I want to trek down under in New Zealand and Australia. I want to stand under the frigid night sky, in near total darkness, the exhaust that is my expelled breath rising like puffs of tiny clouds past my eyes as I stare up into the northern lights, the aurora borealis. I want to glide on a bullet train through Asia, and ride the passenger rails through Europe. I want to walk through African villages until I reach Lake Victoria and then head out across the Serengeti. I want to tuck my grandchildren into bed and give them a good-night kiss while their mom and dad travel on some romantic getaway. I want to write a novel and know that it touched at least one person. I want to see an angel fly, his wings at full span, his body on a high rise, on his way into the heavens, until he sees me staring up at him, and he changes course and comes back down, lands softly in front of me, smiles, and says, "Hi, Brian."

I have a big bucket. Inside it is a long list. I know I will not do most of the things on my bucket list. I know that a lot of it, perhaps most of it, is just dreamy, wishful thinking. I have as much chance of doing most of my bucket list things as I have of winning the lottery. Twice. And you know what the oddest thing is? I think the oddest thing is that, if what I believe is right, if what *you* believe is right, the thing that I most want on my list, the thing that sounds like the craziest thing on my list, may actually be the thing I am most likely to see. In this life or the next. An angel. All my life, I have wanted to see an angel.

So, I suspect, did John. What do you suppose was on John the Revelator's bucket list? Do you think he wanted to check off visions of slaughter and seas of glass and fields of Armageddon and hordes of apocalyptic horsemen and cycles of plagues devastating the earth and torturing its inhabitants? Do you think he wanted to check off having seen 666, the beast from the sea, or its disciple, the false prophetic beast from the land? I can't imagine he wanted any of that. What John had on his list were churches in trouble. He had Christians in danger of losing their Christlike identity. Some of them were so pure that they harshly judged and condemned their fellow believers. Some of them were so lukewarm that they refused to stand up and testify to the faith they claimed to cherish. All of them were itsy-bitsy, little, Lilliputian-like communities, with tiny numbers of believers, whose fragile house churches cowered like dwarfs alongside the gargantuan temples to the Greek and Roman gods and goddesses. No, on his list, John checked off helping churches and church people.

Because once upon a time, *John's time*, there *was* a dragon. . . .

John saw a struggle between death and life. Desperately does death desire to devour life. Theologian Pablo Richard says the woman John sees in the sky is a sign of life. She is pregnant, about to give birth.[1] The woman has twelve stars on her crown. Twelve probably represents the number of the tribes of Israel, the people of God. She *is* God's people, . . . about to give birth to a male child who will shepherd the world with a rod of iron, a fierce and faithful determination. According to Psalm 2, this child will be God's Messiah.[2] The Messiah represents the promise of life that God would one day bring to this death-dealing, death-obsessed, death-wearied world.

The dragon is the sign of death. It has many ancient names. Python. Tiamat. Leviathan. Satan. Commentator Mitchell Reddish says: "He is each of these—and all of them combined—for he is the representation of all that is evil and in opposition to God."[3]

John's life-and-death struggle story has a clear movement. The pregnant woman appears in the sky. Tracking her, the dragon follows, hoping to devour her child. When the child is snatched to heaven, the woman goes to ground on the earth, hoping to escape. The dragon chases the child into the heavens, to destroy it. To destroy the child is to destroy the hope that this world infested by death can ever be transformed into a Reign of Life.

It is, presumably, the dragon's hunt for the child that ignites chaos and ultimately war in heaven. Everything that happens now happens from heaven's side to protect that child! I suspect that it is here, in this delicate moment, with the life and death of God's Messiah, and perhaps the life and death of God's people on the line, when John wishes that he, too, could see an angel.

Right on cue, Michael, no doubt wings at full span, soars into and across heaven. With his magnificent rise comes the dragon's stupendous fall. To earth. Where the woman has escaped. Unable to get the first child, the dragon now hunts the woman and her other children. They would be us. This story is John's way of explaining to *us* why our world is the way that it is. A draconian force has entered our history and our world and pursues our people and our faith. Our earth story begins where the dragon's heaven story ends, with a magnificent, mythical monster standing on the seashore, surveying the human horizon, awaiting the reinforcement of historical beasts who will come in the form of human governments, agencies, individuals, situations, and circumstances to finish the fight it has started. If it cannot get the child, it will devastate the people who gave birth to it. That people would be us. A people who John believes are in trouble. Everything that must happen now must happen from the church's side, our side, and must happen to protect God's people.

Because God's people and God's world are in trouble. We talk about the rise of secularism and the fall of faith. We fear a world that seems without focus or direction. We mourn for people who seek a spiritual connection with God and a communal relationship with God's people and end up instead feeling lost and frightened and alone. How did our world get like this? How did our church get like this? How did God's people get like this? It was at the moment of asking this question that John's mind flashed back to a dragon.

When I was growing up, and I would do something wrong, my mom would ask me, "Brian, why did you do that?" Man, that question would annoy me. What child knows why he does something that, upon further reflection, was clearly one of the more stupid things any reasonable person would ever have included in his portfolio of things to have done? Two hours earlier, in the bravado of the moment, with my two brothers looking over my shoulder and all power residing in my person, it looked like a kinda cool thing to try. Who can answer why he and his brothers try to catch what they think is a baby copperhead snake in a gooseneck juice bottle? It seemed reasonable at the time. The snake was there. That was the quickest jar we could find. And who wouldn't want to have a poisonous snake in a jar to haul into his house? Why would I do that? How do I know? So, why would she keep asking me why?

I started thinking of a stock answer because I had to say something. She kept asking the question, so clearly she wanted an answer. In the end, because I was in church all the time and the preacher kept telling me all the time that we were all sinners, I thought about saying, "Because I'm a sinner." But I was smart enough to realize that might sound too much like a mockery of myself, a mockery of her question, and a mockery of our faith, so I translated it into, "Because I'm bad." That worked the first time, and the second time. It seemed to appease her. But then my brothers started working their way into my business. It's not like I was out thinking up stupid stuff to do and they were sitting on the angelic sidelines watching me blow up my little world. They were right in it with me. And they were also getting the same question. So they started answering, "Because I'm bad." And my mom caught on. Once when I threw out, "Because I'm bad," thinking that the old confess-I'm-a-sinner answer would appease her divine wrath, she flipped the script with the most outrageous use of grace I had at the time ever heard. She replied, "No you're not, you're not bad, you're a good boy, a wonderful young man. So tell me why would a smart, good young man do that?" Well, who has an answer for that? If you can't say you're bad, if one of the powers that be is convinced you're good, then you've got to figure out why you keep getting caught up doing bad stuff.

John was trying to figure that out on a cosmic scale. He wasn't worried about me trying to catch a snake in a juice jar. He was trying to figure out why the world, the world God had created good, kept getting caught up doing bad stuff. Why was the world and the people God had created good so messed up? Why were the church folk God had called to be God's disciples, to witness to God's lordship, hounded with the threat of persecution for making that witness and were therefore trying their best to figure out how to get out of making that witness? How did this happen? How did the good cosmos get so crazy, contentious, chaotic, and ultimately cataclysmic?

It was about *that* time in John's deliberations that a sign appeared in heaven. A dragon. *A DRAGON!!!*

That dragon who possesses institutions and people and infects them with a brokenness so severe that it maims, mutilates, and murders countries, communities, churches, and individuals, their hopes and their dreams, *THAT DRAGON* is just one of the reasons reasonable people dismiss the book of Revelation. *After all, there is no such thing as a dragon.* No such thing!!! Not in Rwanda. Not in Baghdad and Sadr City and the Sunni Triangle. Not in Darfur. Not in Somalia. Not in

Mali. Not in North Korea. Not in Iran and Afghanistan. Not in Syria. Not on the West Bank and the Gaza Strip. Not on the U.S.-Mexican Border. Surely not *in* the United States. Not in someone's broken heart or shattered spirit. In *our* world, the *real* world, there is no such thing as a dragon. No such thing.

As I ponder John's story, as I ponder our own situation in the world, and even our circumstance in the church, the broader Protestant and Catholic church, and the more specific Presbyterian church, gasping and heaving as it struggles against the weight of its own theological determinations about who is right and who is wrong, and threatens from the pressure of it all to rip apart, I meditate on the cautionary words uttered by the cartoonish villain of the silly movie *Pirates of the Caribbean*. As the moonlight hits him and betrays his true, ghoulish identity, Captain Hector Barbossa warns Miss Elizabeth Swann, the woman he has kidnapped and locked up in the brig of the pirate ship, the *Black Pearl*: "You best be believin' in ghost stories, Missy. Cause you're in one." John is all but certainly telling those of us who read his Revelation: "You best be believing in dragon stories, Christian. Cause you're in one."

For John the question is not, "Is there a dragon?" The question is, "Who is going to fight the dragon?" And *that* is where the angel comes in.

Once upon a time, there was an angel. . . .

Michael fights against overwhelming odds. The power of the dragon is mammoth. The heads, the diadems, the horns. So massive is it that even its tail can sweep a third of the stars from the sky. Michael is just Michael. No description of his greatness. He's just an angel. Taking on a dragon. With God. We can be sure that Michael does not fight alone. In fact, we can probably assume that the power of victory lies not with Michael but with God. God fights *through* Michael when Michael fights *for* God.

As Michael gazes at the breach of heaven's defenses, at the place where the dragon has invaded God's space, I wonder, . . . does he weigh the daunting odds? Does he become mesmerized by the challenging statistics? Is he terrified and paralyzed because of how mighty the dragon appears? Is he furious because while all draconian hell is swirling about and threatening to destroy the heavens and therefore their world, John's seven churches are calm and serene, in their sanctuaries, partaking of their communion, singing their hymns like "I've got peace like a river in my soul"? Is he annoyed that while the dragon is on the prowl in the world, staking its claim to the people who populate and power the planet, the Christians are arguing with each other in the church? Is he worried that the odds are against his shaking the churches sufficiently out of their spiritual slumber and their theological theatrics to engage the brokenness of the world around them?

We focus on the statistics, how big the problems are, how little we are, how broken we are, how some Sundays we go to church just to be with each other in the faith and other Sundays we go to church just to beat each other over the head with the faith, how sometimes we are so connected in church that you cannot tell us apart, and other times we are so obsessed with our pious principalities and priestly powers that we tear ourselves apart.

The dragon knows it has the upper hand. Sometimes we know it too. Small churches. Poor churches. Unhealthy churches. Split churches. Polarized society. Wandering souls. Homeless hearts. Broken people. Damaged, threatened, chaotic, potentially cataclysmic world. *The dragon commands the statistics, and therefore the dragon has the edge*. Not us. Like it was once even in heaven. When war broke out *even* there. And yet, with a great red dragon sweeping a third of the stars from the heavens, poised to devour even God's holy Messiah, Michael steps up before God's throne and defiantly declares, "My Lord and my God, I report for duty."

And the Messiah? Where was he? Reporting for duty? Doesn't look like it. It looks like he gets off easy. He appears to have had his own personal rapture. While Armageddon breaks loose in heaven, he appears to be in some sanctuary somewhere safe and secure. Such an appearance deceives. Because his duty station was the cross. In John's story world, while Michael was fighting in heaven, the Messiah was fighting on the cross. He suffers there. He dies there. But he is not devoured there.

He is resurrected.

God wins by snatching Jesus, by raising Jesus from the dead. Resurrection is God's ultimate weapon.

And that is why the promise from God is that there will come another resurrection, which will be modeled on Jesus' resurrection. When God finally takes over this human world and this human history and makes it God's own world and God's own eternal time, God will do it the way God finally did in the dragon, through resurrection, but this time, the resurrection of all the dead who will rise up into a new heaven and a new earth. The statistics say, "Death wins. Every single time." The Resurrection says, "Hold on. Not so fast . . . "

In the meantime, while we wait for that final, ultimate resurrection of all the dead, we are called to rise up with resurrection faith, with resurrection promise, with resurrection power and witness in *this* time, our time, *this* history, our history, against every injustice, oppression, and brokenness, within the church and without, that is the manifestation of a draconian infestation of our world. To witness for the Lordship of Christ is to witness against evil in any form, institutional or personal, it takes. We don't do it alone, as Michael did not do it alone. We do it by appealing to the world transforming messianic victory of the resurrection. That is the call. This is the moment. Sign up or step aside.

Once upon a time, there were believers who actually *believed* that they were called to fight like angels. John says, "They conquered the dragon!" That ought to be us! Michael's call is our call. To rise up through the statistics, through the difficulties, and through the hopelessness as though resurrected by faith, to engage the world and transform the church. That is why this seminary has been here for 200 years. That is why this seminary has been tasked with shepherding the leaders who shepherd the church. That is why this presbytery is here, why it has been tasked with shepherding the shepherds. For 200 years we have been on station. Together. Our duty and our joy is finding ways to continue following the resurrection call for the next 200 years.

John wants his followers to see their struggles as more than just everyday struggles. And even though they are just small groups of tiny house churches, he wants them to believe that they can change not only the life of one lost soul, but that they can also transform the brokenness of an entire world. As tiny as his people are, he wants them to believe that they can take on the opposing greatness of even a draconian Rome and win. Because what they do, they do with and for God.

Some of us are old enough to remember the classic movie scene where Rick and Ilsa are about to part for what will be forever. The conversation goes something like this:

ILSA	But what about us?
RICK	We'll always have Paris. We didn't have, we, we lost it until you came to Casablanca. We got it back last night.
ILSA	When I said I would never leave you.
RICK	And you never will. But I've got a job to do, too. Where I'm going, you can't follow. What I've got to do, you can't be any part of. Ilsa, I'm no good at being noble, but it doesn't take much to see that the problems of three little people don't amount to a hill of beans in this crazy world. Someday you'll understand that.

John, for some reason, does not understand *that*! John believes that our problems, our words, and our deeds *do* matter. Because they are not just our problems, our words, and our deeds: they are part of God's problems, God's word, and God's deed in challenging the draconian force that threatens human existence at every level. Do you hear that? When we parishioners pay our pledges, commit our time, and sacrifice ourselves; when we youth group members grow our faith into a life of determined discipleship that bleeds mission; when all of us think much and do more about resurrecting people and circumstances that are near death in our schools, communities, and churches—then, as witnesses for the resurrected lordship of Christ in an un-Christlike world, *we* are combatants in God's war, on God's side, as God's resurrection kingdom knifes its way into our death-obsessed history, fighting its way against the forces of the dragon that would break that kingdom and destroy the people who would populate it. What John wants to tell his churches and us today is this: every moment you live, every decision you make, every class you teach, every worship service you attend, every baptism you celebrate, every church you encourage, every office assignment you staff, every effort you engage, makes you more like Michael than you know.

Be like Mike! Go after the dragon. Wherever it is. Whatever it is into.

That is our call. Our call is not to sit passively in the pew or loiter too long in the library. Our call is to witness as Michael witnessed in heaven, as Jesus witnessed before the cross, on the cross, and especially after the cross. Our call is to stand up and say something, stand up and do something, stand up and change something. Reconnoiter the situation, gather up your resources, ratchet up your resolve, call out your crew, step into the moment, and say, "My Lord and my God, I report for duty."

And maybe years from now, when those who follow us look back at Union Presbyterian Seminary and the Presbytery of the James, and the Christians who populated them, they will be motivated to proclaim: "Once upon a time, there were angels. . . ."

Chapter 3
Preaching Paul
Apocalyptic Vulnerability

A popular television series debuted in the fall of 2010: *The Walking Dead.* Its premise is simple. A sheriff, is wounded in the line of duty. Seriously injured, he slips into a coma. During his period of incapacitation, a ghastly pandemic breaks out in the world. An unspecified, rabidly contagious virus destroys the higher functions of the human brain and leaves a hollowed-out, violent, attacking, corpse-like entity in its place. For all intents and purposes, persons infected by the disease are dead. And yet they are still animated, still in some sense alive. The series traces the exploits of the, medically speaking, "resurrected" sheriff and a small remnant of survivors as they try to escape both the walking dead and the virus that has created them. Theirs is a world that has been invaded, occupied, and terrorized by death. Death's utter defeat of their world appears imminent.

Paul, according to Galatians 1:11–24 (see also Acts 9 and 22), has his own odd, one might even say apocalyptic, awakening. While the Galatians version contains none of the theophany-like appearances of blinding light and thundering voice narrated in Acts 9 and 22, the autobiographical report does suggest that some extrahuman revelation forced itself upon Paul, compelling him to "wake up" and see the world and his place in it differently than he had before. It is not just that his cause takes a wild and fairly incomprehensible shift from persecution to promotion of the Christian faith. His understanding of God's actions in Christ reconfigures everything about his comprehension of the human historical era. Through his conversion experience, he has awakened to the realization that his world and the people who walk it are infected by the virus of Death. Paul clarifies our circumstance and God's response: invasion of the dead. Death has invaded. God has invaded in response. God will very soon vivify the dead. Then the dead, too, will invade.

AN APOCALYPTIC PAUL

Like John of Patmos, Paul is an apocalyptic thinker and writer.[1] A brief and cursory appeal to citations from the apostle's letters makes the point dramatically. First Thessalonians 4:15–17 not only showcases Paul's belief that Jesus' return is imminent within his lifetime; it also indicates that this precious moment will signal a rapturing of believers, living and dead, to meet Christ in the clouds. In her wonderful work *Our Mother St. Paul*, Beverly Roberts Gaventa observes:

> First Corinthians celebrates the coming destruction of all God's enemies (15:24–28), and Rom. 8 pits God's power over against that of all the forces that attempt to separate humanity from God's love (also see Rom. 16:20). The Philippians hymn anticipates the bowing of all creation 'in heaven and on earth and under the earth' before the name of Jesus (2:10).[2]

As Richard Hays notes, even Galatians, though it lacks reference to a specific apocalyptic scenario, "must be understood as 'a letter fully as apocalyptic as are the other Paulines,' because it reveals the present as the time of 'the dawn of God's

New Creation.'"[3] From the beginning of his apostolic mission to the end, Paul's thinking, teaching, writing, and indeed his very essence are steeped in apocalyptic eschatology. Indeed, as Gaventa rightly notices of Galatians 1:11–12: "Paul announces emphatically that the [very] gospel he preached came by means of apocalypse."[4]

J. Christiaan Beker is therefore right to conclude that Paul's "apocalyptic can neither be eliminated nor reinterpreted in such a way [as] just to accommodate our tastes and sensitivities."[5] But that does not mean that contemporary scholars and preachers do not try to do just that. Gaventa argues that "whatever Paul may have believed, contemporary Christians cannot find themselves in this cosmic apocalyptic battleground. The shadow of Rudolf Bultmann's insistence that the New Testament be demythologized lingers."[6] We contemporary preachers are often more Bultmannian than we know. Perhaps, in the end, we are also more Corinthian than we would like.

A useful historical conversation revolves around Karl Barth's inspection of Paul in his classic little work *The Resurrection of the Dead*. Allow me a moment to refresh the particulars of his points and the debate it generated. In this study of 1 Corinthians, Barth centers Paul's thought in chapter 15, where the focus is on the resurrection of the dead. Chapters 1–14 comprise the ethical mandate for Christian living. Paul lodges the apocalyptic imperative behind these ethical mandates in chapter 15. Correct Christian behavior is based upon a correct Christian understanding of the resurrection of the dead. Barth, though, starts to back away from apocalyptic eschatology in his dialectical approach to biblical interpretation. He argues that while Paul is indeed speaking of last things, the apostle does not mean the end of time as the literal termination of history, but the qualitative end that marks all of time that precedes it.

Bultmann, reacting to Barth, argues that there *is* literal apocalyptic language in 1 Corinthians 15, but declares that it is not Paul's primary concern.[7] Bultmann instead centers Paul's focus in chapter 13. For if Paul is really using apocalyptic eschatology to give support to the letter's ethical mandates, then, for

Bultmann, the climax of the letter must be in its ethical core.[8] Love, the central focus of chapter 13, by its juxtaposition with chapter 15, is shown to be the ultimate possibility for human activity because love has become an eschatological event. For the demythologizing Bultmann, the preaching of love *is* the resurrection of the dead.[9]

Ernst Käsemann noticed that something like this dehistoricizing, demythologizing, and therefore delegitimizing had occurred centuries earlier in Corinth. He argues that Corinthian eschatological enthusiasm was distinct from both the eschatologies of Jesus and the Palestinian Easter communities that succeeded him. Neither the expectation of an imminently inbreaking reign of God nor the theological relevance of a reign that was already immediately present were evident. Eschatological relationship with God, what we colloquially often refer to as "salvation," was instead, for this Gentile community, collapsed totally into the present. The resurrection of the dead, in its symbolic essence and qualitative impact, had already taken place. The logical conclusion to such a line of thinking? Any literal, future resurrection of the dead, an embarrassment, was discounted and denied.

This discounting, perhaps denial, but certainly downplaying of a literal, future resurrection of the dead brings us back to dehistoricizing, demythologizing, remythologizing, and eventually to us: mainstream and academic Christians. It is all about *us*! The apocalyptic focus on the cosmos and its literal end-time rehabilitation via a universal, transformational Dawn of the Dead degenerates into a fixation on redemption from individual sin. The concentration is less and less on God's future intervention and the urgency that God's future intervention places upon our efforts for present preparedness. Instead, we perceive our salvific state, which in apocalyptic eschatology is out there in the future and only in God's sovereign purview, to be more and more not only *presently* realizable, but in some tangible ways under *our* theological control. And so Beker argues, "The imminent triumph of God in Christ is here translated into our human responsibility in Christ."[10] Thus we focus on correct doctrine, right belief, and appropriate behavior because *that* is what saves us, and we judge others more harshly when their doctrines, beliefs, and behaviors differ too radically from our "orthodox" own. In such a moment, having rendered impotent the silliness of a future intervention marked by a literal, great gettin'-up morning for all the dead—something only God can make happen—we are left with this qualitatively present, eschatologically realized sense that the end is no real end at all. Instead, *the end* becomes a qualitative marker of God's ultimacy that lives itself out *in the present* as love and as the proclamation of the Christ kerygma. Beker sums it up well enough: "Our prevalent way of overcoming the difficulty of Paul's apocalyptic seems to lie either in the solution of realized eschatology or in that of salvation-history."[11] For perhaps more sophisticated reasons, and with admittedly better ethical results, we *are* as fervently nonapocalyptic as the Corinthians *were*. And so even as we—along with Paul, Barth, Bultmann, Käsemann, and the legion of New Testament scholars and preachers who have followed in their wake—heap homiletic and academic derision down upon the Corinthians' aberrant, Greco-Romanized, pseudo-Christian lives, in those moments when we realize just how apocalyptic Paul was and how apocalyptic we mostly are *not*, we cannot help but usefully conclude that in the fullness of this ironic circle of faith, we are, all of us, Corinthians now.

We, like the preconversion Paul and the postconversion Corinthians, do not fully appreciate the magnitude of the mess we are in. Our homiletic task is to shake our congregations out of the slumber that makes the dream of the ultimate, end-time prize seem like something they already hold in their present congregational and individual grasps. We have all heard the pious, self-righteous, it's-all-about-me Christian question, or some variant of it, that presumes an affirmative answer: Are you saved? The right answer is a universal negative: No! Nobody, absolutely nobody, is safe!

Where the combat circumstance of the reign of God is concerned, there is no such thing as "quality time," as if there is some essential, more important time that we spend with the one we love that makes up for all of the literal, quantitative time when we ignored her. Where this present era is concerned, there is no linear, literal time where we find ourselves subjected to the powers that rule this age—and an exceptional qualitative time where the faithful, the so-called "saved," live beyond the reach of those powers. There is present time and there is future time. There is this age and there is God's age. In this age, it is time for us to wake up to the realization that we are living *dead.* That, in a colloquial nutshell, is Paul's apocalyptic point. And that is the starting point for apocalyptic Pauline preaching: *we* are the Living Dead!

WE ARE THE LIVING DEAD

Paul operates from the mythological, apocalyptic categories of life, living dead, dead (type A), and dead dead (type B) that I delineated in the opening chapter on John of Patmos's apocalyptic imagery. Paul even expands upon Death's characterization as an animate, personalized, anthropomorphized power.

In Paul's Letters, type A death, the reality that snuffs out human existence in this historical era, is relative enough, fluid enough that one can rise above it. Jesus certainly does (Rom. 1:4; 4:24; 6:4–5, 9, 23; 7:4; 8:11, 34; 10:9; 14:9; 1 Cor. 15:3–4, 12–23; Gal. 1:1; 1 Thess. 1:10; 4:14). As the firstfruits of a broader harvest, Jesus is the prototype for a subsequent general resurrection (Rom. 4:17; 1 Cor. 15:12–23; 2 Cor. 1:9; Phil. 3:11; 1 Thess. 4:16). In this general end-time raising, we will be constitutionally distinct from the existence we have before we experience type A death. As Murray Harris states, when Paul speaks about a resurrection from the dead (Phil. 3:11) or of the dead (1 Cor. 15:42), he is not talking about the revitalization of dead corpses. "Rather, he has in mind the emergence of deceased persons from the realm of the dead in a transformed bodily state."[12] As with Jesus, so with us: something materially different from what has existed in this historical era is raised up beyond type A death.

Jesus' resurrection further demonstrates the complexity surrounding death for Paul. In Romans 6:9, Paul indicates that Jesus will not only rise beyond death, but that because of this rising, Death, as a power, will also no longer have dominion over him. Death, then, is more than a phase of existence; it is also a suprahuman force that uses type A death as a weapon against even Christ. So Death uses death to exercise authority and control. For a time, even Christ was caught in Death's snare. Even Christ died type A death. It is a death, according to Romans 6:9–13, intimately connected with another animate, personalized, anthropomorphized Power of this age that has captured human beings and battles God: Sin.[13]

Having risen beyond type A death, according to Romans 6:9–13, Christ will never die again. The implication is clear. There is a type B death that is final.

The category opposite type B death is life. It is what Christ receives following his resurrection. Life is direct eschatological relationship with God. Type B death, as its opposite, must then, by definition, be eschatological separation from God. In this historical realm, Christ was subject to the powers of Sin and Death. Christ died the type A death that Sin and Death wield in this age. But Christ was raised to life, eschatological relationship with God, and thus is forever beyond the orbit and control of type B death, which no doubt is Sin and Death's ultimate weapon. What mechanism did God use to destroy the grasp that Death once wielded over Christ? The weapon of resurrection.

If Christ's situation is fairly clear, ours is fairly murky. We who occupy this historical era do not possess life since we do not have a direct eschatological relationship with God. Vulnerable to the influence of Sin and Death, we, like Christ, die a type A death. Based on the fact that Christ's resurrection is billed as the firstfruits of something broader to come, after dying type A death, we have a promised resurrection opportunity for either Life (Rom. 2:7) or type B death (2:8). Type A death is a fluid reality: we will move beyond it. For all intents and purposes, it appears to be a way station and not a destination. We know then precisely where we are going: first, type A death, unless of course the general resurrection happens while we still exist in this historical era; then, second, either life or type B death. What we do not fully appreciate is where we are now. As I have suggested already, according to Paul's theology, we are citizens in the realm of the living dead.

Our cosmic condition is completely characterized by death because it is ruled by the powers Sin and Death. Before Christ's resurrection, humans were so enslaved to Sin and Death that we were open to and vulnerable to no other person or power. Not even God. We were constitutionally of the dead and thus open only to the call of Death. In this state, there was not even any struggle. The living dead live out death easily and naturally because Death is not only the power that rules over us, death is also the circumstance of our existence, the ontological essence of our being, and thus Death's calling voice is the only summons that we *can* hear. We are slaves to Sin and Death precisely because we are the living dead. Dead is who we are. Dying is what we do.

In our preaching we must help our communities get over the conceit of living, the hubris that we are alive. We believe this conceit gives us blanket responsibility for creation. We act and decide with the power of life even though we are not alive. Viewed apocalyptically, life comes *after* the resurrection of the dead. Not before. We are too conceited, too full of ourselves and the life we are certain we possess to realize that we and our groaning creation are in the *before* time. The time of death. In our preaching, we must find a way to, as Paul once did, get this deadly point across.

The opposition in the pews will cry out that when God created humankind in Eden, God breathed "life" into human beings and thus made them "alive." I do not contest the point. Paul explains, though, that in the expulsion from Eden something more precious than a ground lease was lost. Humankind lost "life." In the first human's trespass, all humans die (Rom. 5:12–21). Given Paul's declarations about the rule of Sin and Death in this age, it seems appropriate to conclude that Paul is not talking about a future type A death, which is a natural part of living, but a metaphorical death—akin to type B death, eschatological separation from God—that is experientially real in the present. Paul uses the language of enslavement to describe it. According to Gaventa, "Paul needs the relentless argument of [Rom.] 1:18–3:20 in order to show the depth of human oppression by suprahuman powers."[14] We are slaves to Sin and Death. We are locked into this grisly, cosmic condition. To paraphrase the apostle with what I think is more precise grammar, given the preponderance of aorist verbs connected with human death and dying in this important section: "In Adam, we all died." Ours is an animated, "living" death. We are, all of us, even all of us Christians, dead people walking.

Does this recognition not help explain why we consume each other and our world the way we do? Does it not help us understand why so often we are so vicious with one another on both individual and communal levels? Does it not help us realize why we feel so caught off guard when someone does something truly magnanimous and sacrificial on behalf of someone else, particularly when it is someone unknown? We are dead; it should not be surprising that we behave in such deadly ways.

To use the popular culture's symbolism of *The Walking Dead*, Adam's trespass set off a pathogenic viral release that went immediately global (Rom. 3:23).[15] More than global, it went cosmic. The key apocalyptic point for Paul is now this: because of Adam's trespass and the virus it released, "the cosmos (i.e., the human population and indeed the entirety of creation, . . .) has been taken captive by anti-God powers."[16] Paul graphically depicts the gravity of the situation in Romans 5–8, a section that, in Gaventa's words, "teems with the language of conflict."[17] The imagery is that of weapons (6:13; 13:12), enemies (5:10; 8:7; 11:28), prisoners of war (7:23), and the doubt that there can be peace and reconciliation between warring parties (5:1, 11).[18] Gaventa's conclusion is striking: "[Infected] humanity actually belongs to Sin and its partner Death as its slaves, as citizens of territory occupied by these ruling powers, as weapons in its hands, and thus even as enemies of God."[19]

Every effort humankind has made to check the gruesome contagion responsible for this cataclysmic circumstance, where humans become dead automatons striking out even against their Creator, only made the situation worse. Paul labels the pathogen that Adam's actions released: Sin. And 100 percent of the time, infection by Sin leads to death, not just type A death, but also death of a B type that occurs even while one continues to exist in the historical era. Sin takes up residence and metastasizes in human flesh—not to be equated with our biological tissue, but with the physical essence, the metaphorical, bodily stuff of our humanity—and warps and disfigures it, until we are inhuman, grotesque caricatures of the uninfected bodily entities that we were intended to be. This is the condition I want to describe as living death, which renders humankind the living dead. Given this kind of destructive scenario of apocalyptic proportions, it is no wonder that humans sought an antidote. Paul labels it "the Law." As God's gift to the people of Israel, the Law was intended to assist God's people in adhering to God's expectations for life. But Paul appeals to a forensic argument about the Law in order to show that it leads to hopelessness. The Law cannot deliver (Rom. 2:12–16; 3:10–20, 19; 4:15; 8:1; 7:17–8:8).[20] This is because the living dead, enslaved to Death by Sin, did not have the facility to capitalize on the Law. Sin captured and twisted the intended antidote until it became more harmful than useful; it pointed out just how "dead" humankind was to God's expectations for life, but did not provide humankind with the power to overcome that deadness. Thus like a malformed vaccine, the Law ended up worsening the condition of human deadness, reinforcing it, rather than curing it.[21] Through the Law, Sin thus trapped humankind into this living death. What Paul, formerly a champion of the Law, wakes up to is the realization that there is no miracle cure, no potion, no vaccine that can check the power of Sin and therefore overcome human enslavement to Death. This is how humans become the living dead.

One cannot, as humans found out with the failed Law experiment, treat this Sin-deadened existence with medicinal research, litigate it through forensic skill, or overcome it by providing a perfect human whose ethics other humans may be exhorted to emulate. The situation is that of an occupation by a foreign power whose viral rule is a product of our own human—Adamic—failing.[22] We dwell in a land of the living dead. We, too, *are* the living dead. We are in the dark here. Help must come from outside. Someone must invade this territory, engage the conditions that have been imposed, and topple the ruling powers that imposed them.

A FOCUS ON RESURRECTION

Which brings us to God.

How, exactly, does God invade and engage?

Käsemann has made the case that the transforming intervention was built around the "expectation of an imminent parousia."[23] Beker has reaffirmed that God's pivotal invasion is Christ's parousia and the resurrection of the dead that comes with it.[24] While Martinus C. de Boer agrees that Paul emphasizes Christ's parousia (cf. 1 Cor. 15:24–28), he also believes that there is something more: "Paul applies 'apocalyptic language' not only to the End and the parousia, but also to the gospel he now proclaims and the faith it creates. The gospel and faith, which take their point of departure from Christ's death and resurrection, are also part and parcel of Paul's apocalyptic eschatology."[25]

J. Louis Martyn has pioneered this line of discussion by suggesting that while Paul certainly looks out to the imminent future, the apostle's apocalyptic focus is much closer to his historical home.[26] Working from Galatians 1:4 (Christ's self-giving sets "us free from the present evil age"), Martyn recognizes an apocalyptic, revelatory shifting of the ages—from enslavement to the powers of Sin and Death to freedom from those powers, which has occurred with Christ's death. In this way, the cross is as purely apocalyptic as revelatory of God's end-time goal for humankind, as is also the coming parousia.[27]

God's apocalyptic weapon appears to be the cross. One could certainly get that impression from both Paul's own comments and the conclusive remarks of his many interpreters. At 1 Thessalonians 1:10, Paul argues that Jesus, whom God raised from the dead, rescues us from the wrath that God directs toward Sin and Death and those enslaved to those powers. But the emphasis on the resurrection as the principal invasive act retreats when Paul definitively declares in Romans 5:9–10 that God has moved decisively through the blood and death of Jesus on the cross. Indeed, at 1 Corinthians 2:2, Paul emphasizes this crucifixion focus: "For I decided to know nothing among you except Jesus Christ, and him crucified." In retrospect, focusing on letters like Galatians and 2 Corinthians that are oriented primarily around the death of Christ, scholars from Augustine to Luther, Calvin, Barth, and Bultmann have proposed so narrow a focus on Golgotha that Beker can call their thinking an "exclusivistic theology of the cross in Paul."[28] Indeed, Gaventa observes that it is the crucifixion, not the resurrection, that occupies center stage in the all-important Galatians correspondence. "Do Paul's references to the cross carry an implicit reference to resurrection as well, as is sometimes suggested? The answer to that question, at least in Galatians, must surely be no."[29]

Martyn, citing especially Galatians 1:3–4, appeals to Paul's fight in Galatia with gnostic enthusiasts who championed a superlative spiritual sensibility. They claimed no longer to live according to the flesh (κατά σάρκα), but according to the Spirit (κατά πυεῦμα).[30] Paul, working from God's invasive maneuver of the cross, insists that the transformation is not one of living in this era according to some spiritual enthusiasm, but living in this world according to the cross (κατά σταvρόυ). It is through the cross, then, that we are snatched out of the grasp of the powers of "the present evil age."[31] The cross becomes the turning point in the war between the ages. Because of the cross, as Martyn points out, "the marks of the new age are at present hidden *in* the old age."[32]

From this Galatians starting point, Gaventa widens the cross's field of operation throughout Paul's Letters. Building from Romans 3:21–26 and 8:31–32, she argues that Paul "explicitly identifies God's offering up of Jesus Christ in death as the apocalypse of God's gracious defeat of Sin. As God once handed humanity over to Sin, God has now handed over the Son Jesus Christ for Sin's defeat (1:24, 26, 28; 8:32)."[33]

No wonder, then, that the call for apocalyptic Pauline preaching and liturgy is often a call for a more provocative preaching and celebration of the cross. So Larry Jones and Paul Sumney write: "We may want to throw the 'blood hymns' out of the hymnal and to keep our crosses golden and pretty, but apocalyptic thought forces us to see, even on the heavenly Lamb of God, the marks of slaughter."[34] The end result is, as Beker has realized, the preaching of a cruciform life, a life dedicated to living out the marks of crucifixion in our own daily experience. The Christian way becomes a path of suffering and sacrifice. How do we get here? Forensics. Again. Having failed to make forensics work with the Law, we try our best now to make it work with the cross.

De Boer's analysis of the cosmological and forensic categories is useful. In the cosmological category, the created world has come under the dominion of evil powers. God will invade the present world and defeat those powers. The only questions are when and by what means.

In the forensic category, cosmological forces are absent. The emphasis is instead on freewill and individual human decision and the sin of disobedience against God that develops as a result. Death is a punishment for this fundamental sin. God provides the law as a remedy. The key conflict is imaged in terms of a courtroom rather than a battlefield.

According to de Boer, like the Dead Sea Scrolls, Paul's Letters employ both patterns. Paul appeals to forensics in the Adam story (Rom. 5:12–21; 1 Cor. 15:21–22, 45–58), but he is also very cosmological (Rom. 16:20; 1 Cor. 5:5; 7:5; 2 Cor. 2:11; 11:14; 12:7; 1 Thess. 2:18). In the end, though, de Boer believes that Paul trends toward the cosmological: "Thus, while such passages as [Rom.] 8:1 and 8:33–34 indicate that forensic categories have hardly been given up or left behind, the structure and progression of Paul's argument in Romans 1–8 suggest that motifs proper to cosmological apocalyptic eschatology circumscribe and, to a large extent, overtake forensic motifs."[35]

This cosmological trending begs a provocative question: what really is the key apocalyptic weapon in God's invasive arsenal? De Boer concludes that it is the cross even though, on the surface, it appears that the cross is an explicitly forensic maneuver. After all, the notion of the cross—at least on the surface—appears to be one of justice satisfaction, not contested territory invasion. So Douglas Campbell declares: "The Father graciously sends the Son to accept the despairing individual's deserved punishment through his death on the cross. The demands of justice from the cosmic ruler for the punishment of wrongdoing have thereby been met, as that punishment has rather cunningly been redirected, and this of course is the origin of the model's theology of atonement."[36]

Campbell is concerned about several logic flaws in this forensic approach to the cross. His principal concern seems to be that there is something unjust about such a transfer of punishment. And in any case, how is it that one person could pay for the wages of sin for all humankind? Here the church has often turned to the theory of Anselm, who argued that because an offering of unlimited value was needed to atone for such an enormous amassing of sins, only the death of God could provide sufficient compensation for the sins of the world. God incarnate must therefore die. In this way, sin could be properly accounted for, forensically speaking.

De Boer chafes at this schematization precisely because it is *too* forensic. Yes, he says, Paul does include this version of God's actions in the cross, but only because of his context and the imagined Roman Christians who naturally understand the cross as a forensic category, and who also cannot separate themselves from the perspectives of forensic Jewish apocalyptic eschatology. "For such Christians, presumably, Christ's death would have been understood as a sacrifice atoning for past sins (Rom. 3:25–26; 4:25; cf. 1 Cor. 15:3; Gal. 1:4). This sacrificial death did not put an end to law observance, but quite the contrary, it obligated those so forgiven to obey it all the more (cf. Matt. 5:17–20)."[37]

But if sin atonement is not Paul's point, what is it? De Boer argues that cross language should be interpreted cosmologically instead: "The meaning of faith is actually determined by the cosmological-apocalyptic disclosure of God's righteousness and of sin in the crucifixion of Christ. Christ's death cannot be understood in exclusively forensic terms, since it marks God's triumphant invasion of the world 'under sin' (Rom. 3:9) to liberate human beings (the ungodly) from sin's deadly power.[38]

The cross as liberating invasion clearly seems to be Paul's understanding at Galatians 1:4. The question is, how, logically speaking, does Paul get there? I do not think he can, *unless* he gets to the cross by way of the resurrection. In fact, one must read 1:4 through the lens of Paul's opening statement in 1:1, where his introductory, tone-setting description of Jesus identifies him as the one whom God raised from the dead. Indeed, this raising is not only how Paul gets into his Letter to the Galatians; it is also how he gets into both Christ and the Christian tradition. Paul moves by way of the apocalypse of the risen Christ; everything, literally and figuratively, starts with the resurrection. Resurrection is the apocalyptic revelation that Christ first uncovers and then uses to transform the way the apostle understands everything in his world. It is not the crucified Christ who starts him on his way; it is the risen Christ who points him back geographically toward the apostles and back temporally to the cross. He may not speak a great deal of the resurrection in Galatians, but one is hard pressed to understand how he gets to Galatians without first having gone through the resurrected Christ. Paul rightly says that he preached nothing but Christ crucified. One might paraphrase him to say that he preached nothing but the *resurrected* Christ who had been crucified.

Paul needs the resurrection to make his formula work. In the logic of his cosmological construction, crucifixion is not an invasive act. In an era ruled by Death, killing someone seems an act more of collusion or surrender than opposition. It remains difficult to comprehend how subjecting Jesus to type A death interferes with the strategic design of the powers Sin and Death, which is to subject everyone to type A death and subsequently the finality of type B death. The countering invasion seems to occur at just the point when, having been killed, Jesus is raised up. It is in this almost magical, certainly miraculous escape from death—and thereby escape from the rules of Death that govern this reality and give the kind of sense to this reality that allows Sin and Death to maintain their control—that Christ reveals the impotence of death, both in its A and B types. In the crucifixion, God plays along. In the resurrection, God reconfigures the game. That seems to be precisely what Paul is himself getting at in 1 Corinthians 15. It is also what George Nickelsburg believes is on Paul's mind when he connects faith and salvation to Christ's resurrection at Romans 10:9:

> Citing the primitive Christian acclamation "Jesus is Lord" (see also 1 Cor. 12:3) and the creedal formula "the God who raised Jesus from the dead," Paul interprets Jesus' resurrection as his exaltation to the status of Lord, and he identifies Jesus' resurrection and exaltation as the event that provides salvation to those who confess and believe in them. Noteworthy in this conditional sentence is the absence of any reference to the salvific character of Jesus' death as an article of faith that leads to salvation. One's faith is placed in the resurrection, which rescues Jesus *from* death.[39]

Why is this discussion so important for the contemporary church and our contemporary preaching to it? Beker cautions that when interpreting the cross, we must always do so in the larger apocalyptic context in which the cross functions. "A focus on the *cross alone*," he writes, "distorts the relation between the cross and resurrection."[40] The death and resurrection must always be seen as dialectical. Beker also believes that they must be seen consecutively. I agree. But I switch the progression. The cross must be encountered, as Paul encountered it, *through* the resurrection. Otherwise, it is incomprehensible, as we learn from the apostles who followed Jesus around

Galilee and Judea. Beker captures the end result of this progression rather well:

> A theology of the cross, then, that is unrelated to the resurrection as the "first fruits" of the kingdom of God and of the future resurrection of the dead encourages not only an individualistic distortion of Paul's gospel but also an exclusivist centering of that gospel on the Christ-event. And so it can chart our future as human beings only in terms of our individual obedience to the cross and of a cruciform life. It has nothing to say about the future of the world or our future communal solidarity in the kingdom of God. The future resurrection of the dead now becomes transposed into a doctrine of post-mortem afterlife for the individual believer.[41]

But is that not exactly where our centuries of teaching and preaching have brought our mainstream churches? To a doctrine of postmortem afterlife for the individual believer? Where everything is about us? What of our funeral sermons with their preoccupation with a life well lived on earth and now well situated, in many ways because of that earthly good living, in heaven? Death is made palatable in the Christian framework because we believe and we preach that we can individually rise beyond it, and we take comfort that those we have lost individually have indeed risen beyond it, and further that we may one day, in our own individual resurrection, get to be with them again. The best *collective* image we can muster is couples and families reunited in God's presence, a family of loved ones, together for all eternity. Though for some dysfunctional families that might seem like the perfect presentation of hell, for most it is the individualized, personalized, postmortem dream. It is this individualized disfiguring of resurrection that, at least in Christian circles, makes death livable.

The counter to such a myopic proclamation of the faith is Paul's presentation of the crucified Christ's resurrection as the invasion of an occupied world, an invasion that is not all about me and my individual future faith relationship or secular standing in the world, but rather about the breaking free of this entire world and cosmos from the grip of powers hostile to us and to God. Yes, that means something for me individually, but it means something first and foremost for our world. Operating from such a resurrection focus, we are commissioned to retrain our homiletic sights away from individual believers and their particular idiosyncrasies, sinful and not, and take full aim at calling our people to participate in God's ongoing invasion, reclamation, and transformation of our world. Our goal, we should preach, is not to die and get to heaven, with our loved ones hopefully trailing in our wake. Our goal, we must preach, is to live into the war raging all about us, siding with God's forceful engagement against the powers that overwhelm this world and its desperate age, even if, and perhaps especially when, the casualty count for believers rises high. This is what it means, it seems to me, to live out resurrection in a world and church preoccupied with crucifixion.

Thus it is the resurrection of Christ, I am arguing, that is the turning point in the cosmological war. It is the resurrection that reveals God's intent for humankind and the cosmos. It is the resurrection that is God's act. The cross, . . . well, that's on us! We are the ones who drag him there, hang him there, kill him there. God is the one, the only one, who raises him up from there. And in the process, God sends a potent, proleptic message and creates a clear circumstance. So states de Boer: "The resurrection of Christ 'from the dead' is in short, as Schweitzer correctly perceived, a 'cosmic world-event, one that marks the turn of the ages.'"[42] God's past invasive act of Jesus' resurrection disorients the rule of the powers of this age and sets the stage for God's final, culminating resurrection of all the dead, which will disempower Sin and Death completely.[43] It is resurrection that marks something new. Death, even a death as grisly as crucifixion, is nothing new. Death, by its very definition, is a part of the old age. What is new, completely alien to this present age, is a true, literal resurrection from the dead. In fact, this catalytic event is so strikingly new that Cook claims it "provoked the imaginative new configuration of biblical symbols" in Paul's Letters.[44] Apocalyptic preaching would follow suit by turning the focus away from dying and squarely onto living.

The resurrection, then, *is* the apocalypse, the revelation of God's intent for the cosmos. The cross is apocalyptic because of the resurrection; the resurrection, by its very nature, stands as apocalyptic on its own. How can we know? The answer lies at the end of time, with the general resurrection of the dead that is prefigured in Christ's own resurrection. The general resurrection will not require the cross. The resulting revelation is this: God's intent is not to consign us to death; God's intent is to break us and all creation, the cosmos, free from death forever. That intent is signaled not when humans kill Jesus but when God resurrects Jesus.

God ante ups in Christ's resurrection. This is the first apocalyptic bid that shatters the grip that Sin and Death have over this entire historical era and the cosmos that inhabits it. God plays the final apocalyptic hand at the parousia, when all the chips are down, when Sin and Death are all in, and so is God, when the exalted Christ returns to this cosmological realm. This is what Paul means to say at 1 Corinthians 15:24–26: "Then comes the end, when he hands over the kingdom to God the Father, after he has destroyed every ruler and every authority and power. For he must reign until he has put all his enemies under his feet. The last enemy to be destroyed is death."

This clear presentation of the end is meant to help us more appropriately understand our present. As DaPonte notes, a "true apocalypse does not have to do with a neurotic obsession to calculate the end of time, but rather it is a perception of the world in light of the knowledge of its end."[45] Between the ante of Christ's resurrection and the final call-up of all the dead at Christ's parousia lies the apocalyptic beachhead on which we currently exist. Christ's resurrection shatters the enslaving power that Sin and Death presently hold over us. The apocalyptic determinism that fates us to such perpetual bondage is broken. Just as in Adam's act of disobedience all humankind died, so in Christ's invasive resurrection all are made alive.

What does this "being alive" in the era of the living dead mean? Resurrection injects life into this historical era (Jesus) and into the future equation (parousia). Resurrection is the vaccine, the antitoxin to the poison of death. Life first quarantines (through Jesus' resurrection) and ultimately kills (through general resurrection—cf., 1 Cor. 15:52) the viral infection (Sin) that makes us the living dead. So, yes, after Jesus' resurrection and prior to the general resurrection, we remain the living dead. But with options! As Gaventa puts it, "Those who are 'in Christ' still die and still experience pain and are capable of sin."[46] And yet, something new has occurred: apocalyptic vulnerability. Vulnerability to God!

To understand what has happened, we must appeal to Pauline anthropology. Who are we? What are we? The metaphor I am using, because of its contemporary currency, is the living dead. Paul calls it "the flesh." So Romans 7:14b: "but I am of the flesh, sold into slavery under sin." R. E. O. White clarifies that "Paul never, like the Greeks, identified 'sinful flesh' with the physical body. For Paul, 'flesh' is a moral concept rather than a material one, a psychological force rather than a physical substance."[47] Paul is not opposing the good spiritual with the evil material. In fact, Paul has a high appraisal of the physical body. The body is dignified by the incarnation, and Paul uses the physical body to image the body of Christ—the church in 1 Corinthians 12. The body is also sanctified as the temple of the indwelling Holy Spirit. It can be yielded to God so its members can become instruments of righteousness. And it is destined to be raised incorruptible.

Flesh is the person in one's totality that is, prior to Christ's resurrection, enslaved to the powers of Sin and Death, and following his resurrection, freed from enslavement.[48] Flesh, then, is not inherently evil. It is more the concept of physical personality. As such, as is earthly existence, it is viewed neutrally (2 Cor. 10:3; Gal. 2:20; Phil. 1:22, 24; Phlm. 16).[49]

But it is in the flesh that Sin finds its opportunity. Sin uses the flesh, the humanness of each of us, as its point of attack. Romans 7:25: "Thanks be to God through Jesus Christ our

Lord! So then, with my mind I am a slave to the law of God, but with my flesh I am a slave to the law of sin."

Because of God's invasive act that is the resurrection of Christ from the dead, there is emancipation. The resulting proclamation is that we are no longer, to use Leander Keck's reimaging, prisoners of war to sin. And yet, we remain vulnerable to its seductive, mesmerizing power. So Paul can declare in Romans 7:15: "I do not understand my own actions. For I do not do what I want, but I do the very thing I hate."

The human person, liberated from the clutch of Sin, for some reason will often still choose the way of sin. This is so because, while the cosmic condition on the apocalyptic battlefield has been shifted, we remain what we were, the living dead. But living dead whose enslavement to the powers Sin and Death has been shattered. So, while we are still stumbling and bumbling across the cosmic landscape of this historical era, knocking each other around and knocking nature down, we do so freely. We no longer *must* obey Sin and Death. But Sin and Death are still out there. Where before they could rely on ownership, they now must resort to persuasion. They must convince the living dead to lumber their way and for their causes. Constitutionally, deadness remains who and what we are. This deadness syncs with the forces unleashed by Sin and Death and pulls us back to death even as we seek life. We remain open to Sin and Death because, even after Christ's resurrection, we remain the living dead. Still, with the new condition comes new opportunity. Even for us.

Though flesh remains open to sin, because of Christ's resurrection and through the presence of the Holy Spirit, flesh is now also open to the call of God.[50] In the wake of Christ's resurrection, God's Holy Spirit, a surprise combatant, invades the apocalyptic battlefield and outflanks the forces of Sin and Death. The whole human person, aka flesh, is suddenly as vulnerable to God as it is to sin. So Paul can say, not I, but the sin that dwells in me—but also, not I, but Christ who dwells in me (2 Cor. 12:9). The living dead "fleshly" person, imprisoned under sin, can also be called to redemption precisely because one's person is suddenly just as accessible to God. Where there was once only imprisonment to Sin and Death, now there is both vulnerability to Sin and Death *and* vulnerability to God. The cosmic war, in this way, finds its way inside us.

How does this happen? Paul's apocalyptic understanding of God's Holy Spirit and our responsive human spirit comes into play just here. White argues: "Despite disproportionate attention given to Paul's teaching on the 'flesh,' there is much to show that he believed equally firmly in the 'higher' elements in human nature that were open to God, 'our Spirit' to which the Holy Spirit bears witness, 'the spirit of the man which is in him' (Romans 8:16, 1 Corinthians 2:11)."[51] It is this reality of the spirit within the human person, the germ of the living within the shell of the dead, that directs the person toward God's influence. The spirit is that part of the human as now opened to and directed to God. As Romans 1 and 2 show, no matter how depraved Paul thought humans were, the depravity was not total, precisely because of the human spirit. Even pagans possess it.[52] It is because of the human spirit that the living dead, responding to their vulnerability to God, can miraculously be moral creatures. Following, and because of, Christ's resurrection, the flesh, energized by the engagement of the Holy Spirit with our human spirit, is opened up to the power and will of God. Paul himself says it best at Romans 8:10–11: "But if Christ is in you, though the body is dead because of sin, the Spirit is life because of righteousness. If the Spirit of him who raised Jesus from the dead dwells in you, he who raised Christ from the dead will give life to your mortal bodies also through his Spirit that dwells in you." What a generous picture of the now-vulnerable to God, living dead!

PREACHING APOCALYPTIC VULNERABILITY

Does it preach? It does if we do not shy away from finding a contemporary homiletic metaphor that reveals the truth that ours is a world occupied by imperial, supranatural powers that, though we cannot see them, are nonetheless real. This is not some outrageous "the devil made me do it," silly, secularized theology, but an acknowledgment that behind the corporate and individual evil stalking our world lie forces beyond human control. It is not that individuals are possessed; it is that the cosmos is possessed, infiltrated, overwhelmed, taken captive. We live under the shadow of that captivity still. While the ability of Sin and Death to enslave was broken in Christ's resurrection and their very existence will be shattered with the coming of the general resurrection (cf., 1 Cor. 15:52) of the dead, today they fight on, seeking to attract through artifice and deception what they have lost the ability to do by fiat: hold humankind powerless in their grasp. In the resurrection, God changed something about the world by annihilating the grip of those powers and reconfiguring the human constitution so that it is as receptive to God as it once was singularly receptive to Sin and Death. Our proclamation is this: the rising of a single dead man did all that. The rising of every dead person at that one man's coming again will confirm and eternalize that.

Our task is to preach about this siege mentality in a secular world that believes all evils have human causes and can therefore be rectified through human progress and reason. What better way to do that than through the symbolism of the walking dead, beings whose freedom has been captured by the pathogen of powers unseen, but who now, through the interdiction of God's resurrection vaccine, though *still* the living dead, are vulnerable to the creative, generative, reconciling pull of life. Yes, there is suffering in this scenario. But not suffering, crucifixion or otherwise, caused by God as a means to liberate our world. It is instead suffering that happens when those who act out of their vulnerability to God stand and face the consuming cannibalism of those who continue to devour our world and each other because of a determined loyalty to war powers who no longer imprison us and whom we no longer must serve. Our proclamation to the church begins here. In this decidedly dualistic framework, choice must be made. So Boeve: "A neutral attitude at this juncture is no longer appropriate. Interruption, as the revelation of God, provokes us to assume a position: we can no longer maintain an indifferent stance to what is going on."[53]

We must, instead, call the church to recognition of our siege circumstance and then proclaim a vision for responding to it, a vision based on this resurrection metaphor of invasion. Caught up behind enemy lines, we remember God's individual past invasion and anticipate God's future corporate invasion by staging invasive maneuvers of our own. If, as Paul claims in 1 Corinthians 15, a follower not trusting in the invasive revelation behind the general resurrection of the dead is no true believer, then a church not acting invasively in this world of the living dead cannot be a true church. As Boeve puts it: "A Christian apocalyptic awareness urges us to become conscious of the irreconcilability of history, to pay attention to the victims of suffering and injustice, to recognise the fear of God and the appeal for reconciliation and justice. It is at this point that catastrophe thinking becomes *crisis thinking*: submission to the interruptive judgement of God over history."[54]

In our preaching we are commissioned, then, to rally our congregants to the realization that, in the normalcy of our historical staging, we exist in a crisis moment, with Death stalking voraciously all around us. The person who is made to see this, to see the walking dead and experience the devastation we walking dead cause, cannot possibly sit still. Released from the war prison, vulnerable to God, we have the response-ability to act. Preaching in this moment calls believers to respond to that vulnerability by participating in what God, through Christ's resurrection, started: an invasion that interrupts the politics of this world, that engages the living dead who defiantly and destructively respond only to their vulnerability to Sin and Death, and interrupts the consequences that they indirectly and that Sin and Death directly perpetrate in our world.

Our proclamation must not end with God's past interruptive act in Christ's resurrection, but must anticipate an imminent future transformation where the type A dead will rise to life and the living dead will be transfigured to life. The goal of such proclamation is neither passive waiting nor code-breaking, calculating countdowns, but anticipatory, present, invasive behavior. So Boeve rightfully concludes: "A restoration of the expectation of an imminent 'second coming' rids history of its quietude and increases the tension; instead of paralysing, it will provide a foundation for the seriousness of a liberating praxis and emphasize the urgent and critical character of human responsibility."[55] Apocalyptic preaching focuses out beyond the present crisis of living death with the expectation of certain hope. Apocalyptic determinism lives in a positive way just here. To refer to the Theodore Parker citation that Martin Luther King Jr. made so famous in his civil rights speeches, this appeal to the certain and imminent resurrection of the dead assures those of us preoccupied with the present that though the arc of the moral universe is long, its bend shall surely be toward God's justice.[56] The second coming and the general resurrection that will attend it are both the present promise and the coming reality of that justice. Our task is to live as invasive representations of that future moment in the present.

The apocalyptic preacher's goal, then, is not only to preach an invasion, but also to trigger an invasion. The apocalyptic preacher's aim must be to convince the hearers that we believers can participate meaningfully in that invasion because we have been made vulnerable to God's power and linked to the movement of God's Spirit. We children of God's past and future invasion must be provoked into restaging that invasion in the here and now. We must because our world, occupied by and preoccupied with death, destroys itself even as we speak. And so Nancy Duff, in her article on apocalyptic ethics, rightfully concludes:

> Although we must be alert to the dangers of enthusiasm, we nevertheless live *now* in that new space created by the powerful invasion of Christ. Living within that new space, we can no longer tolerate Old Age distinctions in the social and political order which oppress and destroy. We refuse to allow the political order which has foundations in the Old

> Age to operate under the slogan "business as usual," because we do not recognize its legitimacy in God's world. It is in that new space created in Christ that the Church is called into being and action.[57]

In other words, the present time is *the* time for us living dead to rise to the moment and the apocalyptic meaning of resurrection.

Chapter 4
Raise the Dead

A Sermon

This sermon was first preached at Union Presbyterian Seminary in September 2012 to a Vision For the Future Conference.

RESURRECTION IN 1 CORINTHIANS 15:12–26

From time to time, when I was growing up, my brothers and I put my parents in a rather dubious position. They had to raise their voices to demand that we lower ours. We would be so loud that if they did not get even louder there was no way we would hear their desperate plea for just two or three minutes of peace and quiet. My brothers and me? I don't remember us being all that fond of peace and quiet. You coop three adolescent boys up in a small house on a long, rainy, whiny, we're-bored-because-we-can't-get-outside-and-play Saturday, and there will be noise. Somewhere round about four in the afternoon, my mother's last nerve was fully exposed like a live, twitching wire that we were poking at with a stick as we ran from room to room, tumbling and tackling, yelling and screaming. We would hear her agonizing supplication: "If you don't stop all that racket, you're going to raise the dead."

The first few times I heard her say that, I thought two things. One, since I had never heard anybody say that before, I thought the saying was original to my mom. I was intrigued by her cleverness: you are so loud, even *dead* people, with presumably *dead* eardrums, will hear you. And you are going to *wake* them up. Well, I was wrong. The saying was not exclusive to my mom. Apparently this saying was in the universal mom handbook. Every mom had it in her repertoire. I was also wrong because, obviously, no matter how loud we got, despite how much my mom protested, the dead were *too dead* to pay attention to my brothers and me. Sooner or later, every child came to this conclusion. Take, for example, this account from one Chip Brown, in his online memoir, *More of Chip's Odd Musings of Life*:

> For years my parents told me that I was making enough noise to wake the dead. This instilled in me the belief that *should* I make enough noise the dead *would* rise and walk around. This is *not* the case as I have tried several times. I have learned that trying this for long periods of time in a cemetery will indeed *not* raise the dead. It will however invoke the wrath of the police. So kids when your parents say, "Stop that racket or you'll raise the dead," remember, they have the dead and the police confused.[1]

The second thing I thought when I heard my mom warn that if you don't stop that racket you're going to raise the dead was, "Well, why is that a bad thing?" To raise the dead, I mean. Jesus did it. See Lazarus. God did it. See Jesus. Paul claims that God *will* do it. See *all* of us. In 1 Corinthians 15, Paul makes the outrageous claim that, centuries later, the Negro slaves musically memorialize in one of their spirituals. For every single one of us, *all* of us, there *will* be a great gettin'-up mornin'. God *will* raise the dead. And, one day, the dead will be us.

Well, the Corinthians do not have a problem with us getting dead. People are dying all over Corinth, day in and day out. What the Corinthians have trouble believing is that dead people can live again. They've got statistics on Corinthian death and dying just like we Christians have statistics on human death and dying. Not a lot of things in this world are 100 percent certain. Death is. Always has been. Always will be.

You might not get born. You might not get rich. You might not become handsome. You might not graduate college. You might not grow old. But you will die. The Corinthians knew this fact and accepted it. They also accepted death's accompanying fact: once dead, always dead.

We Christians have statistics on the death and dying of churches. Recently I read a certain book. One of the authors, David Campbell, a professor at the University of Notre Dame, came to our campus to lecture.[2] The title of the book is *American Grace: How Religion Divides and Unites Us*. There is deadly data in the book. On American Catholics: a church that has suffered serious losses, both to conversion to other faith traditions and lapses in faith. The average age of Catholic converts today: 65. The church is aging and not replenishing. Working conclusion: "Except for the arrival of large numbers of Latino immigrants, the future of the American Catholic church might appear bleak."[3] *Death and dying.* The mainline Protestant tradition fares worse. Campbell and Putnam's research leads them to the conclusion that the outflow of the young from mainline Protestant denominations is as great as the outflow from the Catholic church. And because Protestant denominations "lack the offsetting benefits of high fertility and high immigration," they describe the combination of high losses and low gains as "near-catastrophic."[4] *Death and dying.* Even evangelical Protestants are not immune to this death specter. The demographic advantages of high birth rate and higher retention rate among evangelicals ended in the 1990s, "coinciding with a leveling off and even slumping of the evangelical share of the religious marketplace."[5] *Death and dying.* So whose future vision looks bright in this sea of deadening statistics? *The nones.* These are the people who list themselves as not affiliated with any religion. "After 1990, the volume of nones has risen sharply, especially among the youngest cohorts of adults."[6] That is correct; the fastest growing religious category in the United States today is by far the category of folk who say that they have no religious affiliation at all. *The nones.* Literally and figuratively speaking, we religious somethings are either already dead or arguably dying.

It will be a slow death, though. For those who are worried that American society will become secularized to the current levels of secularization in Western Europe, the authors present data suggesting that "if we are witnessing such a process in the United States, at this rate it will take a couple of centuries to reduce American religious observance to the current European levels."[7] So this dying that is overwhelming us is like a slow, creeping, living death. But it is death. We are dying slowly. Yet we are dying just the same. It might even be that dying slowly is worse than dying fast. Who wants to be living dying? But according to Campbell and Putnam, the church is. Living dying. Like a zombie. Who wants to see a stumbling, bumbling, confused zombie church? Who wants to *be* a stumbling, bumbling, confused zombie church?

And as bad as all that is for us Christian Americans, the Corinthian data, at least the data the Corinthians focused on, was still worse! After detailed, persistent, exhaustive study, the Christian Corinthians concluded that 100 percent of dead people and dead situations stay dead. Talk about depressing!

So, Paul has a problem. These Corinthians, who have already raised all kinds of noise about things like who is the most gifted Corinthian in their church *and* speaking in tongues *and* men sleeping with their mothers-in-law *and* food sacrificed to idols *and* love feasts eaten without any semblance of affection—these same Corinthians are now raising a racket of reason that they hope will drown out *all* of Paul's *unreasonable* resurrection noise. You can live in Christ. You can die in Christ. But there is no way you are going to rise in Christ. To *get* dead is to *be* dead. Forever. Sounds like some folks talking about the church today. To get on the trajectory of death is to *stay* on the trajectory of death.

I saw a dark, brutal, violent movie many years ago. I am not even going to tell you the name of it for fear that some of you might go out and rent it and then blame me for your having watched it. It is about a man and his wife who are viciously and senselessly murdered. A year later, a mysterious black crow appears at the man's grave. And the man rises.

He is not back for long. He has returned with the single purpose of destroying the evil that destroyed him. One by one, this resurrected man hunts the men who obliterated his life. In this dark world, he is a night light, not bright, not shining, but visible and searching and searing. As he dispatches one of the men who killed him and his wife, the stunned killer declares the rational truth that the young man's resurrected existence contests: "There ain't no coming back! There ain't no coming back!"

And yet, Paul claims: Jesus . . . came . . . back. Dead. Yet alive. He came back. When YOU know, and even in the first century THEY knew: THERE . . . IS . . . NO . . . COMING . . . BACK.

Well, if that is right, Paul is telling the Corinthians, then your faith is in vain. That is the faith I preached. That is the faith you accepted. That is the faith reality that is saving you—from the trajectory and the power of death—right now. Jesus came back to fight the power that is Death and the people who have been captured and remain captivated by it, the people who make an alliance with Death and then wield death against their own living kind. Jesus came back to this death-dealing world to hunt down the dominion that is Death and to kill it.

It is an oppressive, imperial world, where the poor stand on the corners of roadsides begging for money because they have no hope of surviving unless someone shares their pity and their resources. *It is* a dark world where the leaders of the people are out to claim more power for themselves and will expose their constituents to all sorts of danger and difficulty to maintain their status and position. *It is* a world where the wealthy live large on one end of the social strata, the poor are crushed on the other end, and the people in the middle are squeezed until they have little resource and hope left. *It is* a world crying out for energetic, energized, entrepreneurial leadership that can find a way to carry a Christ message of hope in the midst of hopelessness, life in the midst of dying, saving opportunities in the midst of damning statistics. *It is* a world where the person who stands up for the oppressed and the struggling, who speaks out against the self-serving and the powerful, gets literally crucified. *It is* the world that killed Jesus of Nazareth. And now, Jesus has come back to restore the balance of power in the way God would have it balanced. Jesus has come back to fight for life in a world obsessed with death. If he didn't come back, everything you believed about him, everything you hoped for from him, it all is in vain.

But he came back!

And one day, Paul goes on to say, I will be a part of it. Union Presbyterian Seminary will be a part of it. *You* will be a part of it. Not just the death and the dying. But the new life and the rising. Jesus' comeback is just the start of an even grander, more unbelievable comeback. Ours! *We, all of us, are coming back!*

Just know, though, Paul warns, one comeback depends on the other. Either both are true or neither is true. God did not raise Jesus if God does not have the power to raise any dead person . . . or all dead people . . . or any dying or dead situation. But if God cannot raise any dead person or all dead people, then, of course, God did not raise Jesus. And if that is the case, your faith is in vain.

Resurrection, the *literal* raising of the dead Jesus in the past, the *literal* raising of all those who follow Jesus in the future, at least here in 1 Corinthians 15, is the cornerstone of Paul's faith infrastructure. WE . . . COME . . . BACK! Believe this. Live this. In life. In death. Even in seminary and in church. In your church!

Why is this message so central? What does it all mean? For Paul, Death is the greatest enemy, literally and figuratively. Even now, as we gather here together, Death is stalking us. Literally *and* figuratively. As in Adam, every human died; we all die. Death lurks just beyond our sight lines, in our blind spots, waiting to jump us or someone we love when we least expect it. Have a vision, a hope for the future if you will. Just know that the future vision of every human, every institution, and every church is clouded by the specter of certain death. *That* is literal.

Here is figurative. What do we do? How do we individuals, seminaries, communities, and churches live with that kind of stress: the stress of knowing that we cannot vision for future life without factoring in ever-present death? In the end, even a people who live by hope must come to acknowledge that there is no hope we will ever escape death.

Jesus did! He came back. He broke through death. In doing so, he destroyed the figurative *and* literal power of Death. And when the resurrected Jesus comes back for the rest of us, our resurrection will destroy not just the *power* of Death, but also the *reality* of death. Talk about a powerful, hopeful future vision. There you have one. Death, literal and figurative, gone forever. That is what resurrection is all about. And that is why, for Paul, the stakes are so high.

If Christ has not been raised, then there is no hope for us. There is no power to break the vicious cycle of death and more death that pervades our reality. No one is coming to help the people begging at the corners of the roadside. No one is coming to help the refugees dragging from one hell to the next. No one is coming to help the fugitives running from the oppression that hunts them. No one is coming for those mutilated by the physical, social, religious, and political toxicity that pollutes our age. No one is coming to help us when our lives or our families or our churches or our communities are being strangled by the depressing statistics that choke our hope and aspirations for a vibrant future right out of us. No one is coming to encourage you when your vision falters. NO . . . ONE . . . IS . . . COMING. If Christ has not been raised, *you are on your own.*

But Jesus *came* back. And the figurative and literal power of Life came back with him. With Jesus, in Jesus, and through Jesus, life is coming hard after Death, and no matter how fast Death runs, Life will catch it and kill it. Even in the midst of literal and figurative death, Life *is* coming. That is the future vision. That is the plan. For you. For my seminary. For our community. For our church. Believe it. More important, *live like you believe it!*

Live resurrection in the present like you are certain resurrection is coming in the future. Fight the resurrection fight. Paul declares that the resurrection fight is a fight we have been given the ability and the obligation to join. If God raises literally, I am convinced that we can raise figuratively. In fact, in this contemporary age of dying and near deadness, I am convinced that this resurrection call is our call. The future vision for our lives, for our communities, for our church starts right here. With us. With us working together with figurative resurrection on our minds.

Paul must have had a similar thought about the Corinthian community. Though they were near dead in their faith, they could figuratively emulate God's literal capability by responding to the reality of Jesus' resurrection and the promise of their own. That is why he spends chapters 1–14 telling them how to live with one another, mapping out for them an ethical blueprint for communal revivification, highlighted by that powerful chapter 13 treatise on love. He is showing them how they can resurrect the vision that he had, that *God still has* for the Corinthian community of faith by the way they live their lives. How they live is a demonstration of their trust in God's resurrection power and what that resurrection power means for our future and our present. For our future, it means we will be resurrected like Jesus. For our present, it means we have a chance to preview what new life with God will look like by the way we live this life here and now. Jesus was raised from the deadness that took him. We have the opportunity, knowing that death is not final, knowing that there is a power stronger than death, knowing that power has been shared with us—we have the opportunity to live in the midst of all the deadness that surrounds us as though death has no power, no hold over us. I think Paul gives them a picture of the resurrection, Jesus' at the first Easter and ours in the future, to incite a commitment to living a resurrected way of life, Jesus' life and our life, in the present. We can believe. And we can act. In resurrection power. In my vision, the future, the hope-filled future of the church starts here. Don't just believe in resurrection. Don't just preach resurrection. *Live Resurrection!*

The fast-food company Hardee's has a commercial about taking the eating of their food seriously: "Eat like you mean it!"

Paul is asking something similar of the Corinthians: Live like you mean it. *Live Resurrection!*

We're talking invasion here. In Jesus' resurrection, God invaded this world occupied by Death and fired the first salvo of Life. In the future general resurrection of all the dead, God *will* invade and put Death down forever. In the meantime we and God's church are here. Paul is asking his folks and us to be a part of the figurative invasion that precedes and prefigures the literal future invasion. The literal invasion is the raising up of the dead at the coming again of Christ. The figurative invasion is what *we* do to prepare our people and our world for that coming. We are, then, on a mission. An invasive mission to strike Life into this Death-occupied, Death-obsessed, Death-wearied world. I'm telling you: *Rise up off your pew and rise out into resurrection!*

What's holding you back? I'm not sure that we really believe in resurrection in this day and age. We talk about it around Easter; we celebrate Jesus and the empty tomb. But still we're uneasy about this business of literal resurrection from the dead, or figurative resurrection from troubled times and circumstances. When things go badly in life, in the church, in the political and social world around us, what is holding us back from bringing stuff back to true life?

In the whole Christian tradition, the hardest thing to believe is resurrection, coming back from the dead. And we extrapolate that into our everyday living. Things that die, things that fail, things that falter, they don't come back. So we don't expend what we have or all that we have to bring them back. God expended all God had to bring Jesus back. From the dead. To instruct us in the whole "bringing stuff back" scenario. Things can come back. We *can* bring things back. If God could bring Jesus back from the dead, trusting in God, we can bring the Presbyterian church back from the resuscitator it seems to be on. If God could bring Jesus back from the dead, we can resurrect hope in the life of a schoolchild who just gives up on ever being able to read and stay in school. If God could bring Jesus back from the dead, we can resurrect a struggling youth group or campus ministry so that the next generation can be as strong in the faith as the previous generations. If God could bring Jesus back from the dead, we can resurrect broken homes and shaken spirits. If God could bring Jesus back from the dead, we can resurrect a communal sense of inclusion in a world tearing itself apart along the lines of political and religious ideology.

GET IN THE RESURRECTION FIGHT!

There is death all around. Literal death and figurative death. People die. Mission efforts die. Committees die. Programs die. Ministries die. Churches die. Denominations die. Seminaries die. But I do not believe that what is dead has to stay dead, or what might be dying has to keep on dying. I believe in stuff coming back. I believe in Life coming back. And I believe in participating in the process.

Have you seen the James Bond movie *Skyfall*? There's a scene where James Bond is sitting tied to a chair, and the villain sits in front of him with a gun pointed in Bond's face. The villain says something that prompts Bond to answer, "Everybody needs a hobby." To which the villain asks, "What's your hobby, Mr. Bond?" To which Bond answers: "Resurrection."

JAMES BOND STOLE OUR LINE!

Resurrection is OUR business. Death is a call to action. It always has been. That is why God responded to the wage of human death by creating the refund of Jesus' life. Through Jesus, because of Jesus, God made resurrection our business. And I'm here to declare that no matter the difficulties, no matter the obstacles, no matter the deadness and dying that explode all around us, if God is in the house and God's people are walking the talk, the business of resurrection is good.

Chapter 5
Preaching Mark
Invasion of the Dead

I found myself staring into this cloud of black smoke where the horde had been. The freeway, the houses, everything was covered by this midnight cloud. There was a quiet, a stillness that, in my mind, lasted for hours. And then they came, right out of the smoke like a freakin' little kid's nightmare! Some were steaming, some were even still burning, . . . some were walking, some crawling, some just dragging themselves along on their torn bellies; . . . maybe one in twenty was still able to move, which left . . . a couple thousand? And behind them, mixing with their ranks and pushing steadily toward us, the remaining million that the air strike hadn't even touched! And that was when the line collapsed. I don't remember it all at once. I see these flashes: people running, grunts, reporters. I remember a newsman with a big Yosemite Sam mustache trying to pull a Beretta from his vest before three burning [figures] pulled him down. . . . I remember a dude forcing open the door of a news van, jumping in, throwing out a pretty blond reporter, and trying to drive away before a tank crushed them both. One [military helicopter] driver, . . . brave, beautiful [desperate],

> . . . tried to turn his rotor into the oncoming [figures]. The blade diced a path right down their mass before catching on a car and hurling him into the A&P. Shooting, . . . crazy random shooting. . . .
>
> I know "professional" historians like to talk about how [the battle at] Yonkers represented a "catastrophic failure of the modern military apparatus," how it proved the old adage that armies perfect the art of fighting the last war just in time for the next one. Personally, I think that's a big 'ole sack of it. Sure, we were unprepared, our tools, our training, everything, . . . but the weapon that really failed wasn't something that rolled off an assembly line. It's as old as, . . . I don't know, I guess as old as war. It's fear, dude, just fear and you don't have to be Sun freakin Tzu to know that real fighting isn't about killing or even hurting the other guy, it's about scaring him enough to call it a day. Break their spirit, that's what every successful army goes for, from tribal face paint to the "blitzkrieg" to . . . what did we call the first round of Gulf War Two, "Shock and Awe"? Perfect name, "Shock and Awe"! But what if the enemy can't be shocked and awed? Not just won't, but biologically can't! That's what happened that day outside New York City, that's the failure that almost lost us the whole damn war. The fact that we couldn't shock and awe [the living dead] boomeranged right back in our faces and actually allowed [the living dead] to shock and awe us! They're not afraid! No matter what we do, no matter how many we kill, they will never, ever be afraid![1]

Mark begins here. In a world, metaphorically speaking, just like this. *Demonic:* "My name is Legion; for we are many" (5:9). *Catastrophic:* "In those days there will be suffering such as has not been from the beginning of . . . creation" (13:19). *Possessed:* "My son; he has a spirit that makes him unable to speak; and whenever it seizes him, it dashes him down; and he foams and grinds his teeth and becomes rigid" (9:17–18). *Murderous:* "'This is the heir; come, let us kill him, and the inheritance will be ours.' So they seized him, killed him, and threw him out of the vineyard" (12:7–8). *Self-destructive*:

"Brother will betray brother to death, and a father his child, and children will rise against parents and have them put to death" (13:12). *Terrified:* "So they went out and fled from the tomb, for terror and amazement had seized them; and they said nothing to anyone, for they were afraid" (16:8). *Apocalyptic:* "When you hear of wars and rumors of wars . . . . For nation will rise against nation, and kingdom against kingdom; there will be earthquakes in various places; there will be famines" (13:7–8). *Hopeless:* "My God, my God, why have you forsaken me?" (15:34).

Mark's narrative is more subtle than the science-fictional account of Max Brooks's novel, *World War Z: An Oral History of the Zombie War*, and yet it must have been, in its own way, on first reading, just as striking, just as disorienting, just as invasive. Mark, too, images a world dedicated to its deadness, determined to order itself in self-destructive ways that, in more lucid moments of self-reflection, seem almost pathologically demonic. Even social-religious gifts like codes of holiness and purity and Sabbath have, in this aberrant age, become warped instruments that hatch rather than heal human brokenness.

God responded by invading. Well before the resurrection of the Christ into the heavens, God's insurgency had begun on the ground with this man whose first recorded words were, "The time is now. The reign of God is at hand" (1:15, my trans.). The Gospel of Mark is a narrative record of the inauguration of this invasive reign.

An image from *The Gospel in Art by the Peasants of Solentiname* evokes the sensibility of this reign.[2] It is a remythologization of a Jesus parable by Nicaraguan peasants living under dictatorship in the 1970s. The protagonist in the painting is a peasant sowing seeds. He is walking in a garden, his right arm frozen in full fling, kernels rocketing from his hand. There are two things that I notice immediately about the world envisioned by the artist. First, the sower is not in an empty, virgin field that awaits first planting. There is already vegetation where he is sowing his seeds. The second thing I notice is that the vegetation and the world that encompasses it are neatly ordered. Everything has been planted with precision. It grows in neat, patterned, almost geometrically designed rows.

It is just now that I notice a third thing. The sower is unnecessary. He is not needed in this world because this world already has everything it needs. It needs no seeds. It needs no order. And then it hits me. The sower is trespassing. He is not only invading a profitably occupied territory; his seeds are also striking disruptively against the garden's carefully manicured patterns. By the very nature of where and how they are targeted, indiscriminately, the seeds will raise up a generation of revolutionary and intrusive vegetation, a new garden, germinating seditiously under the quiet cover of earth, and then, with the suddenness of a spring day popping forth in the middle of a frozen February, blooming, booming, exploding into a cloud of fierce, fractious color.

The image is more striking if one imagines a garden of the dead: a beautifully tended, contemporary cemetery. A magnificent place of repose, like Arlington National, with rows and rows of geometrically patterned headstones. Into this ordered, successful, domicile of death comes a man sowing the outrageous intrusion of life. Imagine such a world once these seeds of life burrow down into the ground, root their way into the dead, and germinate. Only in the religious imagination can one comprehend what is likely, now, to spring forth.

Here is where the Gospel of Mark symbolically begins. In a majestic, priestly planned, scribally structured, imperially ordered garden of the *living* dead. And then, suddenly, God invades. *This* is the apocalypse, the revelation of Mark.

MARK'S APOCALYPTIC JESUS

Despite all the scholarly huffing and puffing across the centuries as to whether the historical Jesus was or was not an apocalyptic figure, the Human One, aka the Son of Man, who invades the narrative of Mark's Gospel with the thesis declaration about the imminent arrival of God's reign clearly is God's apocalyptic agent. What Dale Allison recognizes in the tradition about Jesus is particularly pertinent to the Markan tradition: "If the nonapocalyptic Jesus were the historical Jesus, it is peculiar that so much in the tradition, even so much that is regarded as authentic by those who offer us such a Jesus, can be so easily related to apocalyptic eschatology."[3] Appealing specifically to the Markan narrative, N. T. Wright is even more direct: "Mark has written a Christian apocalypse, in which the events of Jesus' life . . . form the vital theatre in which Israel's history reaches its moment of 'apocalyptic' crisis."[4]

The crisis point is the same cosmological moment of engagement so graphically conceived in Christ's resurrection by Paul and John of Patmos. There are two ages. The present one is controlled by forces hostile to God's benevolent intent. The future one is envisioned by God, where the ability of the powers to possess and thereby enslave humankind has been broken. The turn from the present age to the future age happens in Mark, though, with the ministry of Jesus of Nazareth. In fact, I want to argue that in Mark's portrayal of Jesus, something even more creatively dramatic has occurred. In Jesus' ministry, the future age erupts into the present age. In Jesus' person and ministry, God opens a pocket of the future in the midst of the present.

As a story of apocalyptic incursion, God's future invades through Jesus' present. In Mark, then, the key apocalyptic moment, the signature invasion, need not wait for the resurrection, which Mark downplays in any case by giving it only a scant eight verses, and not narrating anything more than the empty tomb even then. God's future hits the ground the moment Jesus engages John the Baptist at the Jordan and the heavens are torn asunder.

In his book *Preaching in the New Creation*, Stephen Jacobsen traces Mark's apocalyptic moment to chapter 13. Comparing Mark's presentation there to what he claims is a standard pattern of presenting God's movement into our world in Jewish apocalyptic, he notices a significant Markan shift. According to Jacobsen, the Jewish apocalyptic pattern is very recognizable. (A) God speaks or comes forth. (B) Nature convulses. (C) Eschatological outcomes are shown. Appealing to Mark 13:24–27, he argues that Mark adjusts the pattern tellingly. (A) The heavens convulse (13:24–25). (B) The Son of Man comes (13:26). (C) Eschatological outcome appears (13:27). Mark's apocalyptic theophany inverts stages B and A.[5] Into a deadened world, where the sun is darkened, the moon is not giving light, stars are falling from heaven, and the powers in heaven are shaken, the Human One invades. The question is, does Mark set up, not just chapter 13, but all of his narrative this way? From my reading, the answer is yes. John the Baptist operates in a lost world where people must seek reconnection with God, through repentance. Into this context, Jesus invades. In the midst of this context, God invades Jesus (1:10). Mark is provocatively intentional with his vocabulary when he tells us that, at Jesus' baptism, the Spirit descends *into* him, possesses him.[6] At 3:20–22, Jesus' opponents rightly recognize that Jesus is possessed by something inhuman; they blaspheme, according to Jesus, because they proclaim the invasive force to be of Satan, not of God.

Invaded by the Spirit, Jesus then invades the lives of his disciples and tells them he is going to send them out to invade the lives of others like fishers with hooks. Jesus subsequently invades a troubled synagogue with a cleansing. Then, in the first controversy cycle that begins at 1:40 and ends at 3:6, Jesus invades sacred holiness and purity traditions that have become warped by abusive human practice . Right from the start, then, Mark establishes the world as a deadened place into which a possessed Jesus strikes. Through and through, it is invasion incarnation.

What is the goal of that invasion? Eschatological relationship with God. Intermittent. Now. Flashes of the future age amid the present. Mark makes the case provocatively at 2:5, when Jesus acts outrageously by forgiving a man's sins. Not through his death, not through his resurrection, but through his mere word, Jesus offers what the temple infrastructure could not (cf. 11:12–25, esp. v. 17; 13:1–2). The spiritual-eschatological transformation is so complete that it has social and physical consequences. So Ched Myers writes: "Jesus summarily releases him [the paralyzed man] from all debt—hence restoring his social wholeness and thus his personhood, which in turn is equated with the restoration of physical wholeness."[7]

Not recognizing that Jesus is God's invasion of the present age, the scribes are upset because only God can remit debt of this kind. But they are really concerned less about God's feelings than their own. Because they are the ones who are humanly responsible for dispensing the eschatological promise and social-religious effects of this divine prerogative, Jesus' declaration undermines their position of socioreligious leadership. Who needs to go to a ruling authority to find God's forgiveness for sin if someone like Jesus can proclaim wholeness on the street? Therein lies institutional blasphemy. The leaders want people to believe Jesus is attacking God's prerogative when he is really attacking theirs. In Mark's understanding, he is not attacking God's prerogative because he represents God: he *is* God's invasion. In this realm of living death, by his word, he secures, in as visible a fashion as possible, the premonition of eschatological life. He will present more previews in notable texts like the woman with the twelve-year bleeding (5:34), the resuscitation of the dead twelve-year-old girl (5:39–42), and blind Bartimaeus (10:52).

Mark's primary narrative theme is that Jesus' preaching way represents the way of God's future reign. In the various manifestations of that preaching—the healings, the exorcisms, and the radical teachings—God's power invades and transforms the human present.[8] The reign of God becomes, to borrow a modern military phrase, an apocalyptic "pocket of resistance." In a strategic sense this pocket comes from the future; it remains the actuality and substance of the future. Though it is partially realized in a present human circumstance, it is initiated, sustained, and controlled by divine prerogative from its consummate future location. However, in the tactical arena where strategic theory comes alive in practical application, this pocket operates from and depends upon human conduct.

Human performance, in this regard, never *becomes* the consummate reign of God. Instead, it tactically *re-presents* the strategic reality of that reign, particularly as it is portrayed in Jesus' life and ministry.

Mark used Jesus' preaching, then, as the tactical revelation of God's future reign. It was preaching that manifested itself right from the start as sociopolitical crossings of oppressive and divisive cultic, ethnic, and legal boundaries (1:40–3:6). Into his Jesus story, Mark encoded the apocalyptic preunderstanding that God transformatively invades human history. He did it by presenting Jesus as a justice-seeking boundary-breaker who preaches, that is to say, who acts in the name of the coming reign of God. The correct messiahship path to follow, therefore, was not the old one of violent and militaristic revolution against the occupying Roman presence, nor hapless collusion with it. The correct path was sighted through the transformative preaching of Jesus, who spoke of the hope for a new Israel whose leadership was more concerned about justice than tradition, service than lordship, and whose reign was as open to Gentiles as it was to Jews (11:17).[9]

Because the reality and direction of the future—which images the touching of lepers, the inclusion of women, the honoring of the broken, the healing and feeding on the Sabbath, the forgiving of sins, the inclusion of Gentiles into the people of faith—are so decidedly different from the reality and direction of the present, Jesus' eruptions of future pockets into the present ignite instantaneous conflict. The demonic forces that profit from the malformed present howl in defiance. And the people responsible for governing the present fight back with every legal and punitive resource at their disposal. It is this conflict in its final form that ultimately leads to Jesus' death on a Roman cross (cf. 3:6). Don Juel remarks: "The reasons for Jesus' death arise from his conflict with those in charge of human affairs, the religious and political authorities. It is their need to live within the bounds of the law that requires Jesus' execution."[10] In a very real, apocalyptically determined sense, his death becomes inevitable.

Already, then, this early into our study, we glimpse the directive for the contemporary preaching task as it develops from Mark's apocalyptic presentation of Jesus of Nazareth. The goal of contemporary preaching must be the establishment of such beachhead pockets of future life amid the present circumstance of living deadness.[11] We achieve that goal by focusing not on Jesus' death, but on his life.

A FOCUS ON INVASION: RESETTING THE CROSS

Mark's discourse on life begins with the dead. To this point, I have tried to image this Markan understanding of our "dead" predicament thematically. There is also a linguistic case to be made. As for John of Patmos and Paul of Tarsus, "dead" is a cosmic, relative linguistic symbol in the Gospel of Mark. This is clear at 6:14, when the popular conception about death, in specific relationship to John the Baptist, is described. The people believe, and the narrative does not challenge the belief, that in Jesus, John the Baptist has come back from the dead. Apparently one need not wait for the consummation of God's reign to be raised from what I have previously described as type A death. The death that occurs in this age was not understood to be a final state.

In fact, death was relative enough that someone with Jesus' powerful connection to God possessed the ability to overturn type A death himself. In the Mark 5 story about Jairus's daughter, a twelve-year-old dies. So relative is her "condition" that Jesus can refer to it as "sleeping" (5:39). Despite being mocked by the onlookers, he takes the girl's hand and revives her. Donald Hagner is right to remind us at this point that what is happening here is not a true resurrection: "It is important to note that in all of these instances we have to do not with resurrections, but with resuscitations. That is, these people were raised to the old life, not to the life of the new eschatological order, and so they had to die again."[12] Still, with this presentation, Mark makes two key points. First, dead is relative. Second, in this present age where deadness reigns, Jesus' life and ministry offer a glimpse of the future, where death is unable to keep its kills.

Even more interesting are the texts that image not resuscitation, but true resurrection. At 9:9–10, Jesus indicates that he will himself rise from the dead. Clearly, the disciples do not understand what this means; they apparently have an insufficient resurrection context into which they can fit Jesus' promise. Undeterred, Jesus presses this promise of his own resurrection at 8:31; 9:31; and 10:34.

Ultimately, Jesus himself experiences type A death. At 15:44–45, he is described to Pilate as a dead corpse. Clearly, though, according to Mark's narrative, he is not dead dead (type B death), as the mysterious stranger in the empty tomb (at 16:6) declares that he has been raised to life. Jesus lectures on life in the chapter 12 argument with the Sadducees, who do not believe in resurrection. At 12:24–27, Jesus makes clear that after dying a person can be raised to angelic-like life with God, a life that is very different from the kind of "living" we experience in this age (cf. 10:17, 30). Thus by Jesus' pictorial representation here, life clearly connects to eschatological relationship with God. Life, then, is something demonstrably different from what we experience as "living" in this age.

Nowhere is this point clearer than in the teaching on costly discipleship at 8:33–9:1, especially in verse 35, where Jesus declares that those who want to save their lives will lose them, and those who lose their lives for his sake will save them. Jesus is talking about two eschatological ends. Two types of life are being discussed. To try to save one's life in this age will mean the loss of one's life in the eschatological age. To lose life in the eschatological age is to gain eschatological death. Here Jesus is speaking neither of relative life nor relative death. Life and death in this eschatological sense are final states. In this historical age, though we do not have "life," neither are we "dead" (types A or B). We are something else, something for which I have been using the metaphor of contemporary popular culture: the "living dead." Mark's point in all of this? Jesus invades this, relatively speaking, deadened space, this historical age. Why? To create the conditions for obtaining eschatological life. In this way, the Gospel of Mark is a historical record of God's past invasion of the dead, or more precisely put, invasion of this living dead age. While there is a hint of a general resurrection of the dead in the gathering of the elect at 13:27 (cf. 12:18–27), Mark's primary focus is on God's Jesus intervention. "Invasion of the Dead" would be, for Mark, primarily an objective genitive; this historical age, the cosmos, and we humans who populate it are the object of God's concern in Jesus' life and ministry.

What God does is invade, not rescue. In a rescue, the primary objective is the securing of the prisoner/hostage and subsequent retreat to the closest-held safe zone. Rules of engagement require only the amount of interaction with the enemy as necessary to accomplish that exit. Invasion has a different strategic objective: to meet and engage all opposing forces with the aim of creating a safe zone of the entire occupied region. The goal is not to snatch and leave; the goal is to crush, conquer, and claim.

Though military strategists have long recognized the usefulness of overwhelming force, God's Jesus invasion does not utilize that tactic. In their book, *Shock and Awe*, Harlan Ullman and James Wade make the case that "since before Sun Tzu and the earliest chroniclers of war recorded their observations, strategists and generals have been tantalized and confounded by the elusive goal of destroying the adversary's will to resist before, during, and after battle."[13] Strategists have a term for this goal: Rapid Dominance.

> The aim of Rapid Dominance is to affect the will, perception, and understanding of the adversary to fight or respond to our strategic policy ends through imposing a regime of Shock and Awe. Clearly, the traditional military aim of destroying, defeating, or neutralizing the adversary's military capability is a fundamental and necessary component of Rapid Dominance. Our intent, however, is to field a range of capabilities to induce sufficient Shock and Awe

> to render the adversary impotent. This means that physical and psychological effects must be obtained.[14]

In the invasive maneuver that is the life and ministry of Jesus of Nazareth, God opts against rapid dominance and deploys instead the surgical, special force strike of a single combatant. And so, Mark presents his readers with a Jesus who, fresh off of his commissioning at the Jordan, immediately engages demonic, institutional, and human forces who represent the deadness of the present age. In fact, this age is so deadened that Jesus likens it to a house imprisoned by the personification of evil. It is at this point that Jesus likens himself to a single combatant who has come in the night to capture Satan and plunder his evil age as an invasive strike force of one (3:22–27).

In such an invasive maneuver, there will be losses, some of them catastrophic. Jesus, God's agent, is threatened early and often (3:6, 22; 6:3–4; 8:31; 9:31; 10:33–34; 14:1–2, 55–65; 15:1–5). In combat against forces that hold title to an entire age, loss is inevitable. To be sure, as we learn from the critical discipleship section of 8:27–33, where Peter identifies Jesus as the Christ and Jesus immediately qualifies his messiahship with the title Son of Man, Jesus' christological identity is tied up with suffering. And not just happenstance suffering, but suffering borne of necessity, an apocalyptic inevitability. It is inevitable that Jesus will suffer because he is ushering in God's reign. The cosmic forces arrayed against God, and the institutional and human figures they possess, can be expected to put up a fight. Therefore, if Jesus is to succeed in his task, if he is to carry through with his mission on behalf of God's kingdom, he will necessarily encounter satanic, cosmic, and human resistance. He therefore will necessarily suffer. D. E. Nineham writes: "But meanwhile, so long as this world lasted, anyone in it who represented God's realm and its values must look for misunderstanding and persecution from the evil powers and the human beings in their sway."[15] No wonder Jesus struck back so angrily at Peter when his lead disciple rebuked him for suggesting such a necessity. To pull Jesus away from such a path would necessarily pull Jesus away from executing God's invasive design.[16] Jesus, accordingly, identifies Peter with Satan (8:33).

Ched Myers also wants us to recognize that, given the social circumstances, Jesus' apocalyptically inevitable suffering is also *politically* inevitable. The reign of God that Jesus promotes will have as dramatic an impact on the political structures of Palestine and Rome as they will have on the cosmic, demonic forces. Therefore the representatives of those political structures will fight back just as bitterly. "This is so," Myers writes, "because, as the advocate of true justice, the Human One as critic of the debt code and the Sabbath *necessarily* comes into conflict with the 'elders and chief priests and scribes' (8:31). In other words, this is not the discourse of fate or fatalism, but of political *inevitability*."[17] Jesus' death is an inevitable consequence of the degree of this age's political deadness.

Jesus' invasive ministry is both God's act and this age's problem. From 1:40–3:6 on, Jesus' preaching is viewed as disruptive, even seditious. As early as 2:7 and 3:6, Jesus must know that if he continues, there will be difficulty. And yet he continues. His decision to keep preaching, knowing the inevitable response, makes his death all but inevitable too. It is interesting that in his first statement about that death (8:31), he describes it in terms of a political necessity. He will meet the end that seditious, political prisoners usually meet. He will end up on a Roman cross (8:34). How he expects his preaching activities to end, on the cross, should tell us something about the nature of those preaching activities.

The question this ultimately raises for us is, what does all this mean for discipleship and for those of us who preach to encourage discipleship? It means that disciples are called to preach in the present as invasive emissaries of God's future reign. This means preaching the Markan cross and the suffering associated with it as integrally associated with Jesus' invasive preaching ministry, never as an event that stands on its own. Just so, Raquel St. Clair writes: "Jesus' cross, viewed in isolation from factors that caused it, degenerates into a symbol for all suffering."[18] Disciples are not called to suffer or to counsel, through their preaching, the suffering of others. Not even redemptive, sacrificial suffering. Even so, disciples must be taught to realize that invasive preaching, by its very nature, is so threatening to the social and political structures, or should be, that if they keep it up, they, like Jesus, will inevitably suffer. Just so, discipleship suffering should never be the goal. An illustrative example from African American history is instructive. Martin Luther King Jr. can know on the night before he dies in Memphis that he may well die. He knows this not because his preaching ministry has been dedicated to martyrdom, but because, given the social and political circumstances of the age in which he lived, and given the nature of the message he defiantly preached, violence directed toward him was inevitable. To rightly follow King, one would not seek a death like his; one would seek instead to preach, like him, an invasive message of future light in a dark, present age.

In this apocalyptic, invasive scenario, Jesus' crucifixion is part of the fight, the result of the invasion, *not* the invasion itself. The cross is one other component for Mark, an inevitable component, of the invasive ministry and should be interpreted in light of the ministry and not the other way around. The cross does not stand by itself. In the Pauline corpus, I argued that the cross must be approached through the contextual lens of the resurrection. Here in Mark, I maintain that the cross must be approached through the contextual lens of Jesus' Palestinian ministry. In Mark, Jesus does not go to the cross because of a forensic necessity to die so as to pay the debt of human sin. At 14:24, his blood of the covenant is poured out for many, but not, as at Matthew 26:27–28, for the forgiveness of sins, something Jesus has declared himself capable of doing through his ministry and word (Mark 2:1–12). The sole strategic objective of Jesus' engagement is God's invasion of this living-dead era and God's confrontation of the satanic powers that hold sway in this era (3:23–27); the primary focus of the Markan apocalyptic preacher must therefore be a recalling of God's invasion through Jesus, and a calling for an invasion-like discipleship ministry that engages the powers and rulers of our age. As preachers we focus apocalyptic not on the suffering and the dying, but on the living, and more specifically, what it means to live invasively in this historical age.

Why, then, does Jesus command his disciples to "take up their crosses" and follow? This taking of the cross is a cipher for invasion and consequence. Nothing in the Markan narrative would support a reading of taking up the cross as taking on suffering, generally, redemptively, sacrificially, or otherwise. "Take up his/her cross" is thus more likely narratively equivalent to "take up my invasive cause." Or as St. Clair puts it: "The cross represents the pain that comes as a result of life-affirming behavior modeled after the ministry of Jesus."[19] The focus in apocalyptic preaching, then, must always be on the life-affirming, invasive behavior. Never on the cross by itself.

The cross is a historical and narrative connecting pin that holds two key points of the story together: the ministry that makes the cross inevitable, and the empty tomb that makes the cross, from the perspective of invasive combat, ultimately irrelevant.

A FOCUS ON RESURRECTION

All of this brings us back to where we began these lectures: a focus on resurrection, even in Mark, perhaps especially in Mark. There are two primary reasons why the powers that rule this age are defeated with God's invasion through Jesus' life and ministry. The first is a negative. The best opportunity for the powers to defeat God's invasive Jesus strategy was a successful crucifixion that would make Jesus dead, not dead in a relative and transient way, but dead dead, the kind of dead from which there is no return. Who could possibly predict the consequence of a situation where the existence of the moral center of an entire cosmic age is eschatologically ended precisely because Jesus socially and politically embodied the morality of God's future age? There would, however, be high expectations for a logical outcome: eschatologically destroy the center, and one would expect the edges, the followers, to fold. But Jesus was not eschatologically destroyed; he was killed on a cross. In this age, where dead is relative, where, narratively speaking, it is possible for John the Baptist to rebound from a beheading, even a cross killing is, at best, a spurious victory. The cross can only impose type A death. But according to the apocalyptic scenario that Mark appears to be working with, type A death is transient, giving way either to type B death or to life. The cross, however, is connected to neither of those static eschatological realities. To obtain victory through the cross, the powers of this age would have needed to connect it to type B death. Yet there is no mechanism within Mark's Gospel or without it to so position Jesus. If, then, being type A dead is only relative, and type A dead is the only kind of dead connected with the cross, then what real victory could there be in the cross for Jesus' apocalyptic, satanic opponents: human, cosmic, or otherwise? In this apocalyptic story line, the cross may be inevitable, but it seems hardly conclusive.

In fact, theoretically speaking, God's invasion could occur, and in fact does occur, in Mark without a cross moment. To be sure, death (type A) is necessary—it is an obligatory prerequisite for resurrection—but death on a cross? Consider the narrative presentation. God's invasion ignites in that striking moment when Jesus tears into the narrative world and engages John the Baptist at the Jordan. God's invasion flares divine intent for the future when Jesus turns up missing from that tomb. If, theoretically speaking, Jesus had died from cancer, or old age, or a broken heart, the invasive realities of the incarnation and the empty tomb would remain real and viable. The cross showcases more about us than it does about God. It confirms the deadness that writhes within us and fights desperately against the promise of future life that Jesus reveals in his present behavior. Given who humans are—the living dead—and who Jesus is, the representation of future life in the midst of a present age consumed by the influence and power of death, the cross becomes an apocalyptic inevitability. Because of us.

Not because of God. Because of what we are. Not because of who God is. Who God is stands exposed the moment Jesus is revealed as God's Son and God's mission is revealed as Jesus' ministry. Who God is stands clarified the moment the man in the empty tomb alleges that Jesus' promise to rise from the dead and restart his ministry through his disciples has been fulfilled. In Jesus' coming, God is the one who breaks in on the powers of death who rule this present age. God is the one who offers a preview of future life to the living dead who populate this age in Jesus' ministry. God is the one who raises up a working demonstration of that future life in Jesus' empty tomb. In a desperate, futile attempt to counter all of these revelations of "life," the living dead offer up a cross.

The resurrection is conclusive. In Mark's odd presentation, even this positive can only be negatively portrayed: by an empty (negatively occupied) tomb. Contemporary preaching often misses the purpose of the empty tomb because contemporary preaching is hung up on the cross. Perhaps not as hung up on it as Jesus, one might say. Was it not Albert Schweitzer who famously said that the victory, the reign of that great man, was that he hangs upon the cross still?[20] We, I would argue, are more hung up on it than Jesus ever was. While our vision tends to stop there, Mark looked beyond, to the emptiness and its implications for discipleship (14:28).

The empty tomb—especially considering Jesus' passion prediction promises (8:31; 9:31; 10:33–34) and his final promise to meet his disciples in Galilee following his being raised up from the dead (14:28), not to mention the mysterious man's declaration that Jesus has indeed been raised (16:6) and awaits his followers in Galilee—is Mark's narrative metaphor for resurrection. Jesus' resurrection, though, is not the invasive turning point between the ages, and thus not the narrative focus, not even now. The negatively occupied tomb is the focus. And the empty tomb is less about Jesus' eschatological revivification than it is about Jesus' waiting in Galilee for his disciples, who, if they are to live into their narrative expectations, must undergo a figurative resurrection of their identities as disciples.

In Mark, it is the living dead, the disciples in this nontransformed age, who are commissioned to rise up from their fear and follow Jesus to Galilee, meet him there as risen Lord, and reengage his invasive preaching ministry as their own. The narrative surprise in a story where resurrection is routinely expected, confidently predicted, and only briefly, and for all intents and purposes rather matter-of-factly realized, is not that Jesus gets up, but, given all that has happened, that his disciples, either those in the narrative or those outside the narrative reading it, rise to the occasion. More than the blind leading the blind, it would be the living dead invading the living dead. Broken as they/we are, as captivated by the darkness of this age as they/we are, they/we are summoned to be the agents of God's future breaking into the present. I wonder if this is what Jones and Sumney mean to say when they conclude that "*the apocalyptic preacher insists that we must measure ourselves by something ultimate.*"[21] In this Markan case, the living dead are forced to measure them/ourselves by an empty tomb. The way the story ends at 16:8, with men scattered and women silent, shows how the disciples in the story measure down.

PREACHING INVASION

Preaching Mark apocalyptically, that is to say, invasively, begins with this measurement by the ultimate, the future, symbolized at the end of Mark by the empty tomb, narrated throughout Mark by the invasive Jesus ministry. As Jesus demonstrated in his ministry and in his empty tomb the reality of God's future in the midst of the present, so we are called to measure up to the focus and trajectory of the empty tomb, that is, to follow the resurrected Jesus to Galilee and reengage his invasive ministry, to preach expectations and realizations of future eschatological life in the midst of a deadened present, where he started it.

We do so knowing that because Jesus has transitioned from type A death to eschatological life, he has made the ultimate boundary trespass. He no longer opens pockets of the future; he has crossed over into the future. Not a resuscitation, but a resurrection has occurred here. Perhaps this is why the story ends the way it does, with Jesus' negative presence. He is not here, at the empty tomb. As a physical presence, neither will he be at Galilee. And yet, that is where he will meet them, if they follow him there and strike their own charge against the boundaries that separate the present from the future and thereby open pockets of God's future age into the devastations of the present age. If Jesus is now indeed of the future, this homiletical breaking of the future into the present is how they/we will transform his negative presence into a positive social, political, ecclesial, spiritual, physical reality. If he is in the future, the only way we can be with him is to open pockets of the future in the now.

We know, though, from the evidence of Jesus' own boundary-breaking preaching ministry that God's future is shockingly different from the human present. To inaugurate that future by preaching that future will therefore inevitably bring conflict. The sparking of conflict is never the goal of preaching. Neither, though, should anticipation of it cause one to shift the direction or content of preaching. Preaching that anticipates God's future, particularly when that future is so different from the agenda of the historical present, is the preaching that faithfully follows the design of Jesus' Galilee program and trusts in the ultimate victory of God's empty tomb.

In other words, God's future reign becomes, in pocket moments that resist the oppressive direction of this historical age, concrete in our present preaching. Speaking about the consummation of God's reign, Randall Reed is right to caution that "it is only God who initiates and enacts the revolution."[22] But God, in Jesus' invasive life and ministry, has done just that, enacted the revolutionary reign. The endgame has begun. We need not feel the pressure of inciting it, but we are being pressured, and through our preaching must pressure others, to engage the powers of this age as a part of it. We are called to apocalyptic action, to the triggering of future pockets of life, as represented by the invasive behavior of Jesus' ministry, in this historical age of living death. Nathan Kerr is therefore right to argue:

> If the church itself is to be understood as the gathering of that people whose very existence is to be a sign and a parable of the incursion of God's coming reign into this evil age that is passing away, then this missionary vocation must be considered equally constitutive of *ecclesia*. The "church" only ever exists, *ecclesia* only ever "is," as the occurrence of a people which, like Jesus himself, is *sent* into the world, a people whose very life is the gift of participation in this world's liberation and transformation.[23]

Kerr's aim is to empower an apocalyptic politics of mission. I see Mark's narrative as wishing to empower an apocalyptic politics of preaching. The mission of our preaching is to create, in a real and vibrant sense, the reality and impact of God's breach of this historical age. If our preaching is not just that invasive, it cannot reveal God's future intent for this historical age. Apocalyptic preaching does not just speak of God's reign; it must also constitute God's reign, as surely as Jesus' exorcisms, healings, and preaching constituted that reign in the first century.

Preaching Mark apocalyptically means developing a clearer emphasis in our preaching on the social and political as well as spiritual domination of this age by forces hostile to God's benevolent intent. Paul DaPonte describes this domination well:

> When an entire network of powers becomes integrated around idolatrous values and behaviors, we end up with what can be called the *domination system.* A domination system is characterized by unjust economic relations, and oppressive political relations, biased race relations, as well as patriarchal gender relations, hierarchical power relations, and the use of violence to maintain them all.[24]

Apocalyptic Markan preaching is dedicated to "identifying the evils that exist in modern-day domination systems," and positing real-time alternatives based on an assured understanding of what God's future portends and requires.[25] Apocalyptic Markan preaching creates a politically and socially engaged rhetoric whose end-time orientation has a potent real-time transfiguring effect on these domination systems and the structures that uphold them. Day in and day out, hordes of people and communities experience a sense of living deadness because of the way political, economic, and social domination systems crush the human spirit in pursuit of corporate and institutional gain. Apocalyptic preaching sees this crushing as a manifestation of Mark's strong man running the house in this historical age. Our calling, as apocalyptic preachers, is to strike our way into the strong man's house, plunder it, and set its captives free. Our apocalyptic preaching thus focuses as much on human systems as it does on individual human sinfulness.

Preaching Mark apocalyptically, then, means preaching from back to front, starting from the empty tomb, using it as a lens to focus in on Jesus' invasive life. I can think of two immediate, fear-based reasons why we would find such a preaching focus problematic. First, to preach the invasive ministry of Jesus as a successful combat strike validated by the empty tomb is to invite a view of Mark's Gospel that glories in success. Ever since Theodore Weeden's *Mark: Traditions in Conflict*, scholars have quarreled over whether Mark's Son of Man portraiture was a direct countering response to the divine superman perception of Jesus that many of his followers had conceived. Could it be that a contemporary focus away from the cross and onto a successful invasive strike followed up by a validating empty tomb would reenergize a glorified view of Jesus of Nazareth: Jesus as apocalyptic supersoldier? Perhaps. Though it would be a misshapen view of Mark's narrative presentation, I do not discount that such an apocalyptic perspective could be crafted and used abusively. However, a counterpoint of sorts is worth noting. A focus on the cross does not guarantee a glory-less or glory-cautious view. Indeed, across the centuries, Christians have gloried in the suffering of the cross and created a spiritual economy where suffering for Christ brings credits, and sufficient credits buy one a sense of better discipleship than those who do not possess equal suffering credentials. We have gloried in the cross and the sacrificial suffering that goes along with it. More important, we have preached the cross as if God also gloried in it. Why is the cross not, as I think Mark portrays it, a place of regret rather than spiritual pride? Why is not anyone forced to pick up and carry a cross forced into a regrettable and not honorable position? Why do we preach it that way? As I have heard that command of Jesus preached, indeed, as I have reflected on my own preaching of that text, I have heard and continue to hear an unsettling tone. It is as though Jesus, a smile on his face, proud, eager, giving a pep talk before the big game, the mother of all games, in fact, preaches, "All right, boys, it's fighting time. Anybody who would follow me onto the battlefield, take up your cross and let's go. Bring it on, world! Bring it! Bring it!"

Instead, I image a despondent Jesus, declaring with conviction, "I will die soon because of what I believe, because of how I have lived and how I promise to keep on living. Because in my present life I foreshadow a future whose ethics and rules and ways of living with and treating one another are completely different from the living deadness that consumes this world. What I believe and how I live are in conflict with what the powers of this world believe and how they continue to live and force others to live. If you would follow me and my beliefs, you will be in conflict with those powers, too. You may well die, too. But I know no other way to flash God's future back into our present. I am sorry. I am so sorry. But I do not see another way. Regrettably, you, too, must take up your cross, and you must follow."

Second, I believe we are frightened of a preaching world not centered on the cross because the cross is like an anchoring stake in the ground of our faith. Jesus' ministry was so long ago, the Gospel recordings of it so faithfully and theological rendered, that we sometimes have a hard time deciding what was historically accurate and what was not. The discussions on the historical Jesus are so heated and convoluted that we end up feeling less confident about what we know of Jesus and more despondent of our ability to engage with him after reading through the literature than we were before we started. And above it all, Jesus' teaching and behavior are so apocalyptically based as to be a perilous foundation upon which to build in these troubled technological, scientific, postmodernist, secular, cynical times. Albert Schweitzer has already stated the case well enough: "Men feared that to admit the claims of [apocalyptic] eschatology would abolish the significance of his words for our time."[26] Yes, we try to tie him to our own time. But as Schweitzer warned, "He does not stay. He passes by our time and returns to His own."[27]

And with the Markan resurrection, there is nothing except the emptiness of the tomb to hold on to. Tenuous security, that! We typically do not trust what we cannot see, so we idolize what we can see. We can see in time; we cannot see beyond time. Apocalyptic vision, and the resurrection that is so central to that vision, lies beyond historical place and time. It therefore lies beyond our grasp. Like Linus, the Charles Schulz character in the classic comic strip series "Peanuts," we need a security blanket to hold on to in this troubled historical age. And so we stick the pious thumb of one hand reverently in our mouth, while with the other we clutch the cross.

We are fond of saying that the one thing we can know about Jesus is that he was crucified. That one sure thing, that happening of the past, is not, at least on the surface, a natural apocalyptic event. It is a historical event. But our faith is not based on history. I am not sure that our faith can even be based on Jesus' being crucified. If it were, it would not matter if he was not resurrected. Paul, though, was right; if he was not resurrected, then our faith is in vain. Which means for Paul, as for Mark, I believe, the pivot point for faith is the apocalyptic knife-edge of resurrection. To keep from dealing with the resurrection as a literal, invasive combat rupture of this historical age of the living dead, we homiletically pin ourselves to the cross.

What if, seen from an apocalyptic perspective, the cross was not the thing? What if it and its violence were seen from the end-time perspective rather than from our-time perspective. God made God's case not because of the cross. But God made God's case *in spite of* the cross. God did not act *with* the cross. God acted *through* the cross. While the living dead, determined to stamp out Jesus' message and ministry because of the life transformation it threatened, stabbed the cross in the ground, God turned an invasive maneuver in the air. Schweitzer was wrong. Jesus was hung on the cross, but he was not hung up on it. He was taken down and, more important, he was raised up beyond it. We must do likewise in our preaching. Raise our vision up and forward, into the future, where the empty tomb points us, a future that will surely—if we re-present in our preaching Jesus' boundary-breaking, leper-touching, sin forgiving, prostitute-socializing, tax-collector-cavorting, unjust-law-breaking, women-receiving, all-peoples-accepting, empire-challenging ministry that began in Galilee—transfigure our present. Apocalyptic preaching is the courage to let go of the past and present, as important as they are, and ground our world in the future, as Jesus did in his Markan ministry. The presence of the cross draws us back to the past; the reality of the resurrection propels us into the future. It is the same future that Jesus re-presented in his present. It is the future we are called to preach today, not an idealized future but an apocalyptic future that has invaded the present in the life and ministry of Jesus and the empty tomb. A future of life preached to congregations of the living dead. Our task is to focus them on life: resurrected life and all that it socially, ecclesiastically, politically, economically, and spiritually means.

A very simple example. In the scheme of things, we have much larger issues before us, but let me illustrate with this. Today, still, the worship hour in this country remains the most segregated hour. Is that what the future of worship looks like? Does our segregated worship reveal God's future of God's people before the heavenly throne? In the reign of God, will we imagine a men's section over there, a women's section over here, a white people section there, a black folk section yonder, and so on . . . ? Is that God's apocalyptic future for worship?

If it is not, why does our preaching allow it to be the church's constitutional present? Who though, in their right mind, would set about on such a preaching program? And yet, this kind of preaching is what it means to preach God's future life in the midst of a dead now. In terms of social justice, economic equality, environmental care, international politics, you name it, the questions arise: Do we see what such an issue looks like from the perspective of God's future? And if we do see such a future, what are we prepared in the present to preach about it?

When I came to my last lecture on Mark, I used to tell my classes that I think I know why the women at the tomb are afraid. They are afraid of the *good news!* The good news is that Jesus represents God's future in the midst of the present. The good news is that Jesus has left an empty tomb in the past and is headed for a rendezvous in Galilee, where, through his disciples this time, he will start breaking the future into the present all over again. *Good news!* It is this good-news future that frightens them. That frightens me.

In the fall of 2010, I was on a plane traveling to South Korea. I awoke at one point during the flight, a little disoriented, and wondered what time it was. I realized, though, that I was in a transitory state. On a plane for ten hours meant that I did not really have a certain time because I was moving too fast and was therefore never local. It is location in space that gives me my best sense of time. But on the plane I was never at a stationary point, so zones and time were always changing. Even if I had asked the flight attendant what time it was where the plane was at that moment in space, the information would have been practically meaningless for me. I could not do anything with that time. That time had no hold on me. Time for me was therefore in reference points. At that point of my querying, my best reference point was behind me. In the past. So, to keep myself oriented, I kept my watch trained to the time in Richmond, Virginia. This was the only way for me to put "timeness" into concrete terms, to make it meaningful. I thought of what my daughter and son were doing. My daughter was just getting out of school. It was 5:30 p.m. in Richmond time, and she had stayed later than usual for an afternoon yoga class. My dad, who had come to stay with my daughter primarily, was picking her up from school. My mom would have remained at our home, getting dinner ready, cooking something, no doubt, that my son and daughter liked, to take their minds off the fact that their father and mother were traveling far away. And I knew what my school was doing. The students were playing ultimate Frisbee on the lawn of our small Quad. The faculty, who had held 4:10 p.m. meetings, were likely on their way home. My office was closed up, as my assistant had left around 5:00. As the dinner hour approached, the library ramped up to receive its evening patrons. But everywhere else on campus it would be quiet. I knew that reference point. Both temporally and spatially, back there. The reference point gave me comfort, a concrete thing, a concrete place, a concrete and meaningful time that now oriented my life. In fact, it was that past that gave promise to my future landing in an unknown place.

That, it seems to me, is one of the reasons why it is easier to preach the cross over the resurrection. We cannot see and place the resurrection. It is of the future, a rupture in the present, whose reality is from a time we cannot yet imagine. We have not yet been there so we, like the disciples in Mark 9, do not understand it. Not really. But apocalyptic eschatology is telling us that what is out there in the future is more real than anything we have left behind us. It is saying, "Let go of your past, even the cherished past people and past events. Your destiny exists in a future where and when you have never been." While all that you know is in the past, all that you are lies in the future. Your destiny lies in seeing that future and realizing that future in your present. For me, to have been told that on that plane, would have been startling, unsettling, shocking, and threatening.

Threatening. Like the freedom riders marching beyond the past, through the present, on their way to a shockingly different future in 1950s Selma, Alabama, singing the folk song, "Keep Your Eyes on the Prize." As Gary W. Charles, pastor of Central Presbyterian Church in Atlanta, Georgia, preaches, refusing to settle back into the evil of "separate but equal," or to be defeated by the "colored only" laws of the land, though the freedom riders were water-hosed, beaten, and arrested, still they sang:

> Got my hand on the freedom plow,
> wouldn't take nothing for my journey now.
> Keep your eyes on the prize, hold on.
> Hold on, hold on,
> keep your eyes on the prize, hold on![28]

Mark is saying: keep your eyes on the future. And hold on! This fight, this cosmic conflict—it's about the future! The future is where the prize is. Where the resurrection is! Perhaps this is the hope for the church, the future. Not the past, where the crucifixion lies. Not the present, where the church stumbles. But in a prized future different from anything we currently possess. Can we, in our preaching, visualize, concretize such a future? We cannot do it with the cross. We need another image—an image of the future—*now*. A resurrection image.

Preaching God's invasion in Jesus' life, ministry, and empty tomb is like that. Our calling to replicate the Jesus invasion in our contemporary preaching, in pocket moments where God's future flashes into the present, is like that. Here, floating in present time, disoriented by the deadness of the world through which we travel, we are commissioned to locate God and then locate ourselves not via a past landmark but through a future vision. The content, reality, and impact of that future flashes back to us in the life and ministry of Jesus of Nazareth. The preaching of that ministry comes to life when we dare to journey with the resurrected Jesus, who has emptied his tomb of all its past and present sacred furniture and headed back to the future. Back to Galilee.

When I told a friend about this topic, developed for my 2011 Beecher Lectures at Yale University Divinity School, and the risky symbol of the living dead that I intended to use as my point of interpretative reference, she said she had a book for me. I was expecting something theological and hermeneutical. What I received in the campus mail was *The Zombie Survival Guide*, by Max Brooks. In over three hundred whimsical, tongue-in-cheek pages, Mr. Brooks outlines his theory and the practices that develop from that theory on how to survive a zombie apocalypse. How to make do in a world overrun by the living dead.

As I have been interpreting the message of the first Gospel, Mark wants us to do something quite opposite and rather counterintuitive. He wants us—as preachers who have followed Jesus back to Galilee—to instigate, foment, and unleash a zombie apocalypse, a world overrun by living dead people who can and will demonstrate the future life as previewed in Jesus' ministry and anticipated in Jesus' imminent return in their precarious existence in this present age. But, because the powers that rule this age have already unleashed an apocalypse of living deadness, we do not have to create the living dead; we need only refocus and release them. Show them their potential. Demonstrate their vulnerability to the life virus that is God, and get them to willingly submit to it, open to it, after we have, through our preaching, brought them into contact with it.

How to go about it? Between Revelation's Dawn of the Dead in the imminent future and Mark's recording of God's insertion of Jesus into the realm of the living dead in the distant past—between these messages lies the release of the pathogen: Jesus' own resurrection that is the virus of life infecting a world breeding on death. To introduce this virus into this contemporary world is to preach the resurrection through the lens of apocalyptic eschatology. A central part of that proclamation is that those of us who follow Jesus to Galilee, determined through our present existence to reveal God's future way of living—we represent the contemporary strain of that life virus. To put it more succinctly, in between Mark's Invasion of the Dead and Revelation's Dawn of the Dead are all of us! The living dead. Ready to *rise!*

Our Markan preaching task, then, is to wheel our straggling folks toward this idea of Galilee, the place where God's future that is Jesus' past detonates all over our present. For Mark, Galilee is where the living dead walk to find the way to eschatological life, a way of life that, though it attracts the inevitability of conflict and death, is a real-time glimpse of resurrection. What a joy it would be if, with our preaching, we could assist in the provocation of an age, once characterized by the deadness that afflicts its politics, its economics, its religion, and its very being, that now is suddenly hell-bent on re-presenting the promise of resurrection. Imagine it: the living dead orchestrating in the present the reality of future life. Now *that* would be a zombie apocalypse.

Chapter 6
Rise!
A Sermon

This sermon was preached at First Presbyterian Church, Raleigh, North Carolina, on the dedication of a significant renovation of the church's physical plant and addition to it.

RISING IN MARK 5:21–24, 35–43

Why are you here?

I know people ask a lot of rhetorical questions these days. Sometimes they know and you know the answer before they finish asking the question. Does this dress make me look fat? Sometimes they really don't expect an answer; they're just making conversation. Hot enough for you? Sometimes they're trying to make a point. Trying to slide it in without having to argue about it. Are you *really* going to wear that tie? Rhetorical questions don't expect real answers. But I do. My question does. *Why are you here? Why did you come?*

When Jesus walks into the gathering of folks mourning the death of Jairus's twelve-year-old daughter, I suspect most of them are cynically whispering that question under their breaths: Why did he come? *Why* is he here? "What can Jesus do for the dead?"[1]

That question is intended to be rhetorical. They already know the answer: *Nothing*. There is absolutely nothing anyone of us, Jesus included, can do for the dead, except cry. Sure, Jesus has been operating at a level most people can hardly imagine. Healing the sick, curing the blind, undoing paralysis. It is hard enough to believe that someone can do *that!* This past summer, my family took some friends from New Jersey to Monticello, the home of Thomas Jefferson. We listened to a tour guide talk about Thomas Jefferson's Bible. Jefferson meticulously went through the Bible and cut out all of the miracle passages. In his Bible, where there used to be miracle stories, now there were just holes. Because you can believe some things about Jesus, but you just cannot, if you're a modern, scientific man, believe in those miracles. Well, many people could not believe in miracles in the first century, when Jesus lived, either. That means that even before the girl died, when her parents were thinking about sending for Jesus, some of the onlookers, perhaps even the parents themselves, were already skeptical that Jesus could do anything meaningful at all to alter the impending tragedy of their situation.

I suspect that when the little girl's parents sent for Jesus, they were doing what some of us do when the lottery gets to be three hundred million dollars. We buy a ticket. Because, well, you never know . . . it could happen. The odds of winning the lottery, they say, are about the same as being hit by lightning while simultaneously being eaten by a shark. But we buy the ticket anyway, because, well, somebody's gotta win the thing! Take a chance. That's what a lottery is. Chance. That has to be what those little girl's parents were thinking. Chance. A lottery kind of chance.

But even they would have to admit that the chances of Jesus healing their daughter when she was so very sick were already astronomical. The chance of him doing something to rectify her situation after she was dead? Worse than being hit by lightning while being eaten by a shark while getting hit on the little toe by a falling star while flying a spaceship while winning the lottery. There *are no* scenarios for that. You die, you're dead. End of story. End of you. Walking on water is unbelievable enough. Raising the dead? Well, there simply are no words to express the utter incredulity surrounding that.

So, why are you here, Jesus? Why did you come? What is it that you think you are going to do?

We can excuse Jairus for playing this ludicrous life lottery. He is a dad. His little girl is dying. We are not surprised that before he surrenders, he exhausts every single option, even the crazy ones. We are also not surprised that, when he finds Jesus, he expects Jesus to respond positively to his plea. After all, Jairus is not an unimportant man. Mark describes him as a leader of the local synagogue. According to commentator Alan Culpepper, such a figure is "appointed to look after the synagogue and take care of the arrangements for the services there."[2] Chosen from among the elders, his duties are to decide on matters such as who reads the Bible during the service and who leads the prayers. He is in charge of the building, if there is one, and ensures that nothing improper takes place within its bounds. Probably he is also wealthy. An ordinary person's house, if he is so fortunate as to have a house, consists of only one room for the entire family. But commentator Eugene Boring observes that, in this impoverished Palestinian world, Jairus's twelve-year-old daughter has her own room.[3]

An important man like this, we are not surprised that he expects someone like Jesus to respond when he calls. Jesus? Well, Jesus surprises me. I am trying to figure out why he is here in this story, and just as soon as I think I understand, he confuses me. He is here, after all, to heal Jairus's dying daughter, right? So I am surprised when all of a sudden he stops going to Jairus's house in order to deal with a woman who just pops up out of nowhere, a nobody, with no name, whose condition is nowhere near as serious as the condition of Jairus's daughter.

I understand when an ambulance, hearing that the governor is having a heart attack, flips on its sirens and streaks out into traffic to get to the state house as fast as it can. I am confused when the ambulance turns off its siren, pulls over to the side of the road, and lets the paramedics get out to tend to some homeless woman who has fallen off her bike and maybe broken her leg. "Why," I want to ask the paramedics on the roadside, "are you *here*? To get into trouble?"

It does not seem to matter where Jesus is. The Gospel of Mark is only five chapters old by the time we come to this story about Jairus's daughter. But already, one thing is clear about Mark's principal character. Wherever Jesus is, he attracts trouble. Case in point: impurity, the kind of impurity that makes a holy person defiled and gets a holy person in trouble with the leaders of the holy people if he does not avoid contact with it. Lepers. Tax collectors. Sinners. Women. Especially out of nowhere, no name, nobody, bleeding women. But Jesus? Impurity clings to him like lint. He cannot scrape the impurity or the people infested with impurity away from his person. So I am not surprised when, like a robe magnetized by static cling, Jesus draws a dramatically impure bleeding-for-twelve-years woman into direct touching contact. While Jesus is weaving his way through desperate human traffic, cutting off others with less dramatic ailments, so he can reach a dying girl in the nick of time, this woman detours him with her desperate, defiling touch. And instead of reading her the riot act and getting back in the fast lane to Jairus's house, Jesus praises her and then stops everything to have a conversation with her. A massive heart attack in the home of a wealthy, important leader of the people down the street, and the Jesus ambulance has pulled over to tend to this unnamed, unclean, unfortunate woman who has fallen off her bike. Why are you *here*, Jesus?

Maybe he is here to make the point that no one is, by virtue of office, title, stature, or financial value, worth more than even the humblest person in God's eyes. This no-named woman deserves Jesus' attention as much as Jairus does. Or maybe Jesus is here to make the point that God can do anything, overcome any obstacle. And though her chronic illness is nothing like the mortal illness stalking Jairus's daughter, it is clear that while no human doctor has been able to help her, Jesus can. Jesus does. *Without even trying!* Perhaps Mark is trying to make the point that for Jesus no human brokenness is irreversible. And maybe, just maybe, Jesus is *here* with this woman to make the point that his power to heal is a sign of an even greater power. Perhaps Jesus is feasting on these lesser troubles in order to demonstrate that he has the appetite for taking on the greatest of all human torments. Perhaps, like an athlete strengthening his body in the weight room in anticipation of the coming battle on the field, Jesus bulks up in the sick room by beating up on human disease in order to get ready for an all-out war with death.

I wonder whether there is an analogous reason as to why you are here this morning, celebrating the successful conclusion of this new building effort. There is, after all, so much desperation, destruction, and devastation in our world, happening like a heart attack all around us. One might rightly wonder why we pull off to the side of the road to celebrate the renovation of another building while so many lives are being torn asunder. But is what you are doing not somewhat analogous to what Jesus was doing? Is not this building update a part of your bulking up for the task ahead? Because renovating this space so wonderfully the way you have done so is not the real test. Just like Jesus' healing that woman with the twelve-year bleeding was not the real test. Yes, healing that woman was difficult. Yes, this building effort must have been difficult. Yes, her healing was necessary. Yes, if your ministry is to continue to thrive, this building effort was necessary. But rebuilding this building, restoring this property, is only the prelude to, the primer of, the preparation for the life-giving, life-renewing, life-restoring ministry that now will flow out of this building. Having bulked up your property, be sure now to use this property as a resource, as a catalyst for beating down the improprieties of death and deadly situations that wage war against God's people and God's causes. I believe that is why we are here this morning. Not only to celebrate the renewal of a building. But also to anticipate the power that this new building makes in you and for you possible.

As you *have* transformed broken brick and worn-out mortar, you *can* transform broken people and worn-out communities. As you *have* reshaped this entire block by committing yourselves to the revitalization of the structure sitting atop it, you *can* reshape this entire city by committing yourselves to the revitalization of the people and the circumstances that are struggling in your midst. As you *have* reached deep into your pockets to generate the funds necessary to tear down the old structures and raise up this new edifice, you *can* reach deep inside your hearts and spirits and pockets to generate the vision necessary to tear down the old walls and older ways of divisive politics, lackluster mission, bland spirituality, and heartbroken lives that threaten God's people and raise up a loving, inclusive, passionate, spiritual way of being Presbyterian in Raleigh, North Carolina.

Oh, but there are some nonbelievers among us! Nonbelievers who do not believe that we have the kind of healing power it takes to engage successfully the death-dealing realities that daily destroy God's people. Sure, we can take dying infrastructure and raise up a new building, but there is no way we will ever be able to take some community's shattered vision, some person's eviscerated hope, . . . some little girl's dead corpse, and raise up new life. That is the way folks were thinking as they watched Jairus's daughter die. I suspect, having heard the hard news of his daughter's passing, it was how Jairus himself was thinking. Jesus knew it. That is why, after they tell Jairus, "Your daughter is dead," Jesus tells Jairus, "Do not fear, only believe."

The present tense of the Greek verb is very important just now. Jesus is not telling Jairus to *start* believing. He is telling Jairus to *keep* believing. Culpepper says it well: "The present imperative [believe] carries the sense of continuing action: Not a single act, but a steady attitude, of faith is called for. . . . The father has already shown faith by coming to Jesus—now he must go on believing."[4] Jesus is telling him: "Jairus, don't stop now! Don't stop believing now! Jairus, you're just getting started with this believing thing. Don't just believe when it's easy, Jairus. Believe now that it's hard. Believe like you mean it, man!" But the stakes are so high now, the obstacles to believing in Jesus' power are so great now. Hard enough to believe in miracles. Impossible to believe that, once dead, a person can be brought back.

With the help of biblical scholars, we can imagine the scene taking place as Jesus and Jairus come to Jairus's home. Already, by now, the funeral for Jairus's daughter is underway. "In the ancient Mediterranean world, without embalming or refrigeration facilities, the dead were often buried on the day they died."[5] At the funeral were, of course, Jairus's family, broken, no doubt, by grief. There was also the obligatory crowd of friends and acquaintances. As Culpepper puts it: "The father of an unmarried girl was responsible for her burial. 'Even the poorest in Israel should hire not less than two flutes and one wailing woman' (*m. Ketuboth* 4.4), but because of Jairus's status in the community, one can imagine a larger number of mourners."[6]

Yes, you did hear correctly. Not only family and friends, but also professional mourners were hired for the funerals of important folks like Jairus. Usually women, these professional mourners would "weep and wail," stamp their feet, wring their hands, play the flute, beat on other instruments, and beat their chests. Today some larger churches are able to hire professional musicians and singers to help the volunteer church members amplify their sounds and voices. Imagine being a professional mourner, hired by a church to come and amplify the sound of weeping and mourning. Imagine trying to explain that job to someone. "Are you a member of First Presbyterian Church? I see you going there a lot." "Oh, no, I'm not a member. I'm a mourner. They pay me to cry."

Yes, they did pay people to cry at funerals in first-century Palestine. But, . . . no, in situations like the one surrounding Jairus's daughter, they did not have to pay anyone to laugh. Yet they are laughing at Jesus. Given the circumstances, laughter arose spontaneously, and perhaps appropriately. Given all that is going on around him, Jesus still thinks there is something he can do.

She is dead! Done. Discontinued. Definitive. And here comes this guy strolling in with the claim that he can make a difference. Admit it. If it happened today, amid all the deadness and all the grief, if someone strolled in the house and told the gathered family and friends, "I can fix this," you would have laughed, too. Not because it was funny. Because it was unbelievable that someone would have this kind of nerve at this kind of time. The questions would be flashing feverishly through your mind: Who *are* you? What do you think you are doing? Why are you here?

To demonstrate the full power of life over death. Death is not even really death, Jesus is ultimately claiming. Not the death we see and fear, anyway. And that is why he calls it "sleeping." She is not dead. She is asleep. As Boring makes clear, "Death is called 'sleep,' not to pretend it is not real, but to deny that it is ultimate."[7] There is dead. And there is dead dead. Dead dead is when you are separated from God for all time, for eternity. That is the death to worry about. This death, this girl's death, the death we fret over day in and day out, this death is not ultimate. This death is akin to sleeping. From this death, there is a waking up. All of us will one day wake up from it. To make that case, to show it can and one day will be done for all of us, Jesus wakes up this little girl right now.

Stop being afraid of death, Jairus; it is only sleep, Jairus. Keep believing, in spite of death; keep living like you will rise beyond death and all the forces of doubt and betrayal and dissension and dispute and desperation that death inspires in the human spirit. If you live with this kind of belief, so that you are not even afraid of death, then you can and you will do anything. You can and you will rise beyond any obstacle, rise to any occasion.

I suspect that redoing and expanding this building required faith from you. As a church, you had to rise to this moment. You knew there was a chance this project could falter. Your capital campaign might fail to raise the required pledges. The economy might go bad, and people might not be able to fulfill their pledges. But the prospect of the project's dying did not deter you from doing what you wanted to do. Enacting the vision you wanted to enact. Making possible the ministry you want to make possible. Take that kind of believing, that kind of rising, into every aspect of your ministry, and you cannot only change this block: you can also change this world.

No wonder, then, that when Jesus took that little girl's hand, he used the language of resurrection. The language that changes our understanding of our place in this world and in God's presence forever. The word he used was "Rise." "Little girl, rise" (5:41, my trans.). It is the word Mark used when, after her healing by Jesus, Peter's mother-in-law rose. It is the word Mark used when, after his healing by Jesus, the paralyzed man rose. It is the word Jesus used when he called forward a man with a withered hand by telling him to rise. It is the word the angel at the tomb used when he told the women that Jesus had been raised. That is why Jesus is there at that girl's bedside: to raise the specter of life in this atmosphere of death. He is as much there for us as he was for Jairus and his daughter. Jesus' words to Jairus are as much for us as they ever were for Jairus and his daughter. Even, perhaps especially, in the face of death, keep believing in life.

That is why Jesus is here with this dead little girl. It is why Jesus was not there at the empty tomb. By placing Jesus where God places Jesus in these critical, crucial moments, God is telling us to stop responding to death or deadly spiritual, personal, social, political, communal, or church situations by giving up. Respond by rising up. Let me show you how. Let me show you what is coming by what happens with Jesus. Jesus will rise. His resurrection is the promise of your own. His empty tomb is the promise that one day your tomb, too, will be empty. What Jesus does here by the bedside of Jairus's dead daughter is what movie studios do with their upcoming films: Jesus provides a trailer of a coming attraction, a preview of what his future and indeed our future will look like by resurrecting this little girl. She did rise! We shall rise!

Why is Jairus here? To keep believing. To provide an example of what it means, how much it takes, how much it means to keep believing.

Why is Jairus's daughter here? To rise, and in rising now to provide an assurance that all of us will one day rise beyond death, too.

Why is Jesus here? To demonstrate God's resurrection power.

Why are you here?

Sometimes, I wonder, why am I here? I don't mean here in this pulpit. I know why I am *here*. You were gracious to invite me. And I am overjoyed to accept, particularly since I get to follow in a way the footsteps of Dr. Walter W. Moore,[8] someone whom I consider a hero of the faith in the history of Union Presbyterian Seminary and the Presbyterian Church. I mean, sometimes I wonder, why am I here in this kind of ministry, the shepherding of theological education at Union? It is difficult to keep encouraged about the mainline church. It is difficult keep encouraged about the circumstances surrounding my own seminary. Difficult financial situation. Hard to raise money in this environment, as you know. Sometimes I think about how much money I have to raise to realize the seminary's vision, and I break out into a sweat and just start laughing. Giggling out of control.

In those moments, sometimes, I start wishing I had gone into other more lucrative professions. Professions that will always be needed, even in down economies. People being people, people will always be getting into trouble. So we will always need lawyers. Some days, I wish I had been a lawyer. Humans being human, humans will always be getting physically broken or ill. So we will always need doctors. Some days, I wish I had been a doctor. People being outfitted with teeth so they can keep chewing their food will always want to be protecting their teeth so they keep chewing. So we will always need dentists. Some days, I wish I had been a dentist. People being wasteful, people will always be piling up trash. So we will always need sanitation engineers. Some days, I wish I had been a garbage collector. You know, they get to ride on those trucks and are out in the open and they don't have anybody bothering them about budgets and fund-raising and theological disputes. There have been a few times when I have wished I was somewhere else doing something else.

I don't know so much about us, but I do think I know something about God. God will always call people into ministry. No matter what we Christians do to the church. No matter what we Christians do to each other. God will always call some Christians to lead the effort of sharing the good news of the resurrection of Jesus Christ and what his resurrection means for our resurrections. I want to be there for God and for the people God calls to help them build the curriculum and the facilities and the faculty that will equip them for the moment when God sends them into laughing, weeping crowds where death has taken over. That, in the end, is why I am here. Why are you? Here. Ask the question. Find the answer. Then act on that answer.

The answer will lie on the other side of difficulties. Perhaps not as difficult as a twelve-year bleeding, or the death of a little girl, but difficulties nonetheless. In those moments, the meaning of this passage is this: Keep believing. Keep moving. Rise! Don't rise above the difficulties. Rise through them. Rise through the difficulties and so transform them into opportunities for new life, just as Jesus transformed bleeding into wholeness, death into life. Jesus rose through the doubt and the laughter. Erased the doubt. Quieted the laughter. Transfigured a world.

So, what Jesus said to Jairus, I say to you. Keep believing. Don't stop now! Now that you have finished this building, do not stop. You are just getting started. Do not just believe when you're fixing brick and lifting mortar; believe also when you are fixing vision and lifting people. Believe like you mean it, church! And then act like you believe. The way you have believed with this wonderful building project. Whatever difficulties arose—and I know there were some—you kept moving, you kept believing, you kept building. You rose through it all. So, what Jesus said to that twelve-year-old girl, I say to this 196-year-old congregation: *Rise!* Rise not just through budget difficulties, cost overruns, construction issues, and differences of opinion about what should go here, what should be done there. Rise to the occasion that this occasion represents. This occasion represents that when First Presbyterian puts its mind to it, First Presbyterian will put its resources behind it. And when First Presbyterian puts its mind to it and its resources behind it, First Presbyterian can do whatever God wants and needs it to do. You can rise to the occasion and raise a building. Now, go rise to the occasion and raise your community. Raise the people struggling in it. Raise the opportunities for mission in this place and beyond. Raise the hopes of folks hopeless in your midst. Raise the vision of a people who, though they think differently, live faithfully together. Raise the vision of one church continuing to believe that as God has made a difference, a concrete difference in your lives, so also you can and you will make a concrete difference in the lives of people in this city; believe that you will make a difference in the life of this city itself. Rise, First Presbyterian. Take hold of Jesus' hand, keep believing, keep building. Your building project is not over. Your building project has just begun. What you have built here is a preview of what you can and will build out there. So, *Rise!* That is why you are here, in this sanctuary this morning, in this community for the decades gone and the decades to come. To celebrate. And . . . to rise.

Notes

Introduction: Invasion of the Dead

1. J. Christiaan Beker, *Paul's Apocalyptic Gospel: The Coming Triumph of God* (Minneapolis: Fortress Press, 1982), 9: "And so I struggled with the relevance of Paul's apocalyptic gospel for our time, a time in which apocalyptic is either distorted into its Pauline opposite by apocalyptic sectarians or silenced and neutralized by the established church."

Chapter 1: Dawn of the Dead

1. Leander E. Keck, "Death and Afterlife in the New Testament," in *Death and Afterlife: Perspectives of World Religions*, ed. Hiroshi Obayashi (New York: Greenwood Press, 1992), 85. See also Richard Bauckham, *The Fate of the Dead: Studies on the Jewish and Christian Apocalypses* (Leiden: E. J. Brill, 1998), 1: It was mainly in the apocalypses that Jewish and then Christian understandings of life after death developed.

2. Gregory M. Stevenson, "Preaching Apocalyptically," *Restoration Quarterly* 42, no. 4 (2000): 237. "Morality is absolute: there is good and evil, right and wrong, with nothing in between. One cannot seek shelter under the umbrellas of compromise and relativism because apocalyptic calls upon people to make radical choices."

3. Larry Paul Jones and Jerry L. Sumney, *Preaching Apocalyptic Texts* (St. Louis: Chalice Press, 1999), 4.

4. J. Christiaan Beker, *Paul's Apocalyptic Gospel: The Coming Triumph of God* (Minneapolis: Fortress Press, 1982), 36.

5. Jones and Sumney, *Preaching Apocalyptic Texts*, 29.

6. Cf. Christopher Rowland, "Apocalypticism," *New Interpreter's Dictionary of the Bible* (Nashville: Abingdon Press, 2006): 1:191. It has often been thought that there were in Judaism two competing types of future hope: national eschatology (rabbinic texts); otherworldly escha-

tology (apocalypses). "The evidence from the apocalypses themselves, however, indicates that such a dichotomy cannot be easily substantiated. Apart from a handful of passages that are always cited as examples of otherworldly eschatology, the doctrine of the future hope as it is found in the apocalypses seems to be remarkably consistent with the expectation found in other Jewish sources." See also Stephen L. Cook, *The Apocalyptic Literature* (Nashville: Abingdon Press, 2003), 20. "The apocalyptic reign of God has nothing to do with many spiritual assumptions and aspirations typical of religious believers in the Western world." Its focus is not simply on an ethereal realm of heaven with souls enjoying pie in the sky. "Rather, its fervent hope centers firmly on a tangible, physical renewal of the cosmos and natural environment and of humanity and human community."

7. Has contemporary Christianity indeed moved away from an engagement with the apocalyptic eschatology that is so prevalent in the New Testament materials? Scores of New Testament scholars will argue that it has. In his classic *Quest of the Historical Jesus*, Albert Schweitzer states the problem exactly: "Men feared that to admit the claims of [apocalyptic] eschatology would abolish the significance of His words for our time; and hence there was a feverish eagerness to discover in them any elements that might be considered not [so] eschatologically conditioned." Albert Schweitzer, *The Quest of the Historical Jesus* (New York: MacMillan Publishing, 1968), 402. Schweitzer, himself, then went on to become an illustration of the very problem he uncovers. While he famously allows the apocalyptic Jesus to go back to his own first-century time, he holds on to the true and universal message of Jesus that was eschatologically valid, and apocalyptically cleansed, for all time. By dehistoricizing Jesus' thought, he gets rid of the apocalyptic man while holding on to his decidedly nonapocalyptic message. Bultmann, with his program of demythologizing, trashes the mythological husk in which Jesus' message is encased in favor of that universal, existential message itself. Karl Barth does something analogous with his dialectical theological approach. While he certainly champions the resurrection of the dead as Paul discusses it in 1 Cor. 15, noting that correct Christian behavior is indeed based upon a correct Christian understanding of the resurrection of the dead, a claim I also champion, he then dehistoricizes the primary Pauline apocalyptic sensibility. He asserts that Paul is speaking of the last things as the qualitative end, which marks all of time that precedes it, not as a literal end that marks God's invasive movement. See Karl Barth, *The Resurrection of the Dead* (New York: Fleming H. Revell Co., 1933), 109.

8. James H. Moorhead, "Apocalypticism in Mainstream Protestantism, 1800 to the Present," in *Apocalypticism in the Modern Period and the Contemporary Age*, ed. Stephen J. Stein (New York: Continuum, 1998), 72. The reference is to Doyle's story about Sherlock Holmes in *Silver Blaze.*

Mainstream Protestantism has perhaps not engaged apocalyptic because it has mistakenly believed that apocalyptic theology was not directed toward the condition of the mainstream Protestant experience. After all, so the thinking goes, apocalyptic materials were written for communities of faith suffering under the extreme duress of social, political, and even physical persecution.

I believe Randall Reed summarizes a contesting point well: "A historical crisis *may* spark an apocalypse, but it is not required." Randall W. Reed, *A Clash of Ideologies: Marxism, Liberation Theology, and Apocalypticism in New Testament Studies* (Eugene, OR: Pickwick Publications, 2010), 57. See also John J. Collins, *The Apocalyptic Imagination: An Introduction to the Jewish Matrix of Christianity* (New York: Crossroad, 1987), 280: "The Jewish apocalypses were not produced by a single 'apocalyptic movement.' . . . The problems to which these revelations are addressed vary in kind." He goes on to point out such circumstances as persecution, social powerlessness, historical trauma, fate of humanity, inevitability of death.

9. See Beverly Roberts Gaventa, *Our Mother Saint Paul* (Louisville, KY: Westminster John Knox Press, 2007), 84: "Christian tradition offers some horrendous examples of what can happen when apocalyptic visions are coupled with unstable leadership. Yet the latter ought not to prevent our taking biblical apocalypticism seriously, since otherwise those texts are virtually abandoned to their overenthusiastic misinterpreters."

10. Thomas J. J. Altizer, "Modern Thought and Apocalypticism," in *Apocalypticism in the Modern Period and the Contemporary Age*, ed. Stephen J. Stein (New York: Continuum, 1998), 346. Beker is even more sweeping: "Legitimate criticism, however, should not make us complacent or blind to the sad fact that respectable theologies of the established church have continuously dismissed apocalyptic from their own theological agenda" Beker, *Paul's Apocalyptic Gospel*, 28.

11. Thomas G. Long, "The Preacher and the Beast: From Apocalyptic Text to Sermon," in *Intersections: Post-Critical Studies in Preaching*, ed. Richard L. Eslinger (Grand Rapids: Wm. B. Eerdmans Publishing Co., 1994), 1–2.

12. Beker, *Paul's Apocalyptic Gospel*, 11.

13. Rennie B. Schoepflin, "Apocalypse in an Age of Science," in Stein, *Apocalypticism in the Modern Period*, 436.

14. Martin E. Marty, "The Future of No Future: Frameworks of Interpretation," in Stein, *Apocalypticism in the Modern Period*, 467.

15. See Collins, *The Apocalyptic Imagination*, 207: "For Paul, the resurrection of Jesus is not an isolated event. It is not enough to believe that God could raise a privileged individual as he had taken Elijah up to heaven according to the Old Testament. Rather, Christ is the first fruits of those who have fallen asleep, and his resurrection is as fateful for humanity as the sin of Adam had been. . . . In short, Paul argues that the resurrection of Jesus must be understood in the context of a general resurrection and presupposes a full scenario such as we find in the historical apocalypses. . . . Since one person has already been raised the rest cannot be far behind. The end is at hand." Also Donald A. Hagner, "Gospel, Kingdom, and Resurrection in the Synoptic Gospels," in *Life in the Face of Death: The Resurrection Message of the New Testament*, ed. Richard N. Longenecker (Grand Rapids: Wm. B. Eerdmans Publishing Co., 1998), 99: "In particular, the resurrection of Jesus, which is an intrinsically eschatological event, is both the proper beginning of distinctly Christian eschatology and the foreshadowing of the coming resurrection of the dead."

16. Michael Barkun, "Politics and Apocalypticism," in Stein, *Apocalypticism in the Modern Period*, 442: "We are arguably in the throes of the most intense period of apocalyptic activity in recent history." See also Thomas J. J. Altizer, "Modern Thought and Apocalypticism," in Stein, *Apocalypticism in the Modern Period*, 346: "So it is that a flight from apocalypticism has occurred throughout Christian history, but most explicitly in the twentieth century, despite the apparent fact that the twentieth century is so clearly an apocalyptic world."

17. Lieven Boeve, "God Interrupts History: Apocalypticism as an Indispensable Theological Conceptual Strategy," *Louvain Studies* 26 (2001): 196.

18. Elizabeth K. Rosen, *Apocalyptic Transformation: Apocalypse and the Postmodern Imagination* (New York: Lexington Books, 2008), xvii–xviii. Rosen goes on to list HIV/AIDS and the threat of virus on a global scale. At the time of her publication in 2008, HIV/AIDS alone had so far killed an estimated 22 million, infected another 42 million, and she foresaw another 50–75 million infected by 2010. "The threats of viral pandemic and the destruction of the ecosystem are the two conditions

that are not only as potentially dangerous as the nuclear bomb, but also have analogous biblical—that is, apocalyptic—motifs in plague and world destruction" (xix).

19. Barkun, "Politics and Apocalypticism," 446.

20. Stephen D. O'Leary, "Apocalypticism in American Popular Culture: From the Dawn of the Nuclear Age to the End of the American Century," in Stein, *Apocalypticism in the Modern Period*, 401.

21. Cook, *The Apocalyptic Literature*, 59.

22. Ibid.

23. Ibid., 62.

24. Will Willimon, *Advent, Christmas*, Proclamation 5, Series B (Minneapolis: Fortress Press, 1993), 4.

25. David Schnasa Jacobsen, *Preaching in the New Creation: The Promise of New Testament Apocalyptic Texts* (Louisville, KY: Westminster John Knox Press, 1999), 87.

26. Cf. Brian K. Blount, "If You Get *MY* Meaning: Introducing Cultural Exegesis," in *Exegese und Theoriediskussion*, ed. Stefan Alkier and Ralph Brucker (Tübingen and Basel: Francke-Verlag, 1998), 77–97; idem, *Cultural Interpretation: Reorienting New Testament Criticism* (Minneapolis: Fortress Press, 1995).

27. Jonathan Maberry, *Patient Zero* (New York: St. Martin's Griffin, 2009), 20.

28. Ibid., 21.

29. Quoted in Robert Jay Lifton, "The Image of 'The End of the World': A Psychohistorical View," in *Visions of Apocalypse: End or Rebirth?*, ed. Saul Friedlander et al. (New York and London: Holmes & Meier, 1985), 153–54.

30. Ibid., 154.

31. Ibid.

32. Ibid.

33. See http://www.cnn.com/2011/HEALTH/05/19/zombie.warning.

34. Kim Paffenroth, *Gospel of the Living Dead: George Romero's Visions of Hell on Earth* (Waco: Baylor University Press, 2006), 13.

35. Ibid., ix.

36. Ibid., 4. "As the series of movies progresses, this theme becomes more and more prominent: we, humans, not just zombies, prey on each other, depend on each other for our pathetic and parasitic existence, and thrive on each others' misery."

37. Ibid., 10.

38. Ibid., 18.

39. Ibid., 17.

40. Rev. 2:7, eating of the tree of life in the paradise of God; 2:17, holding claim to hidden manna, a white stone, and a new name, all representing a new reality with God; 2:28, holding claim to the morning star, a direct relationship with the risen-to-life Lord in the heavenly realm; 3:5, wearing white robes with names in the book of life; 3:12, becoming a pillar in the eternal temple of God in the new Jerusalem, which is direct relationship with God since God is God's own temple in the new Jerusalem (21:22); 3:21, presence with the risen-to-life Lord at the heavenly throne.

41. And, as the promises that conclude each of the seven letters (Rev. 2–3) demonstrates, one can receive gifts in life as rewards for being faithful in this earthly existence. The presumption is that life, connected as it is to the metaphor of crown and saving, is better than anything experienced in this historical era (cf. 14:13).

42. Given the ethical program of John's narrative, it is an existence that dedicates itself to witnessing for the lordship of God and the Lamb that will earn life (cf. 14:13).

43. Sophie Laws, "Can Apocalyptic Be Relevant?" in *What about the New Testament? Essays in Honour of Christopher Evans*, ed. Morna Hooker and Colin Hickling (London: SCM Press, 1975), 99.

44. Loren Johns, *The Lamb Christology of the Apocalypse of John* (Tübingen: Mohr-Siebeck, 2003), 106.

45. Ibid., 129.

46. Ibid., 130.

47. Martinus C. de Boer, "Paul and Apocalyptic Eschatology," in *The Origins of Apocalypticism in Judaism and Christianity*, ed. John J. Collins (New York: Continuum, 1998), 355.

48. Boeve, "God Interrupts History," 210.

49. Ibid.

50. Jones and Sumney, *Preaching Apocalyptic Texts*, 39.

51. Beker, *Paul's Apocalyptic Gospel*, 118.

52. Roger Booth, *Jesus and the Laws of Purity: Tradition History and Legal History in Mark 7* (Sheffield: JSOT Press, 1986), 90–91.

Chapter 2: Call of Duty

1. Pablo Richard, *Apocalypse: A People's Commentary on the Book of Revelation* (Maryknoll, NY: Orbis Books, 1995), 101.

2. Ps. 2:7–9.

3. Mitchell G. Reddish, *Revelation* (Macon, GA: Smyth & Helwys, 2001), 234.

Chapter 3: Preaching Paul

1. In her wonderful work *Our Mother St. Paul* (Louisville, KY: Westminster John Knox Press, 2007), Beverly Roberts Gaventa works from the definition of apocalyptic eschatology in the *Encyclopedia of Apocalypticism*: "the belief that God has revealed the imminent end of the ongoing struggle between good and evil in history" (80). She is right to follow up with the observation that, based on this definition, "it is hard to see how any reading of Paul's Letters could deny that they are apocalyptic" (80–81).

2. Ibid., 80–81.

3. Richard B. Hays, "'The Righteous One' as Eschatological Deliverer: A Case Study in Paul's Apocalyptic Hermeneutics," in *Apocalyptic and the New Testament: Essays in Honor of J. Louis Martyn*, ed. Joel Marcus and Marion L. Soards (Sheffield: Sheffield Academic Press, 1989), 191.

4. Gaventa, *Our Mother Saint Paul*, 89–90.

5. J. Christiaan Beker, *Paul's Apocalyptic Gospel: The Coming Triumph of God* (Minneapolis: Fortress Press, 1982), 79.

6. Beverly Roberts Gaventa, "Rescue Mission," review of *The Deliverance of God: An Apocalyptic Rereading of Justification in Paul*, by Douglas Campbell, *Christian Century* 127, no. 10 (May 18, 2010): 134.

7. Rudolf Bultmann, "Karl Barth, *The Resurrection of the Dead*," in *Faith and Understanding*, ed. L. P. Smith (New York: Harper & Row, 1969), 80–81. "Now it seems to me certain that Paul in 1 Cor. 15 is speaking of such a closing scene of history, although such speaking is really outside his legitimate concern and intention."

8. Cf. ibid., 94: "Since in the First Letter to the Corinthians the dominant theme is not justification by faith but the temporal life of the believer within time, ch. 13 is the true climax of the letter."

9. Rudolf Bultmann, "Ist die Apokalyptik die Mutter der christlichen Theologie? Eine Auseinandersetzung mit Ernst Käsemann," in *Apokalyptik*, ed. Klaus Koch and Johann Michael Schmidt (Darmstadt: Wissenschaftliche Buchgesellschaft, 1982), 371. "The end events come to pass rather in the preaching of the gospel as occurring events, as an event, in which all are involved, who offer faith in this proclamation and who thus have become new creatures, for whom the

old state of affairs is gone, who already have advanced beyond death in life."

10. Beker, *Paul's Apocalyptic Gospel,* 100

11. Ibid., 61.

12. Murray J. Harris, "Resurrection and Immortality in the Pauline Corpus," in *Life in the Face of Death: The Resurrection Message of the New Testament,* ed. Richard N. Longenecker (Grand Rapids: Wm. B. Eerdmans Publishing Co., 1998), 149.

13. Gaventa, *Our Mother Saint Paul,* 127: "Paul does not confine his comments about sin to human behavior, to sin as misdeeds, omitted deeds, even to perverted thoughts and plans. . . . [It is instead] an upper-case Power that enslaves humankind and stands over against God." Gaventa notes that Paul uses the word family of "sin" 81 times in the undisputed letters; 60 of those occurrences are in Romans, and 42 in Rom. 5–8. Sin is often the subject of a verb: It came into the world, 5:12; it increased, 5:20; it exercised dominion, 5:21; it produced, 7:8; it revived, 7:9; it dwells, 7:17–20.

14. Gaventa, "Rescue Mission."

15. Cf. Douglas A. Campbell, *The Deliverance of God: An Apocalyptic Rereading of Justification in Paul* (Grand Rapids: Wm. B. Eerdmans Publishing Co., 2009), 663: "Verse 23 indicates that the situation of humanity in Adam is *universally enslaved and trapped.*"

16. Beverly Roberts Gaventa, "Neither Height nor Depth: Discerning the Cosmology of Romans," SBL presentation (Atlanta, GA, 2010), 6; also in *Scottish Journal of Theology* 64 (2011): 265–78.

17. Gaventa, "Neither Height nor Depth," 7.

18. Ibid.

19. Beverly Roberts Gaventa, "The Rhetoric of Violence and the God of Peace in Paul's Letter to the Romans," a paper, 11; published in *Paul, John, and Apocalyptic Eschatology: Studies in Honour of Martinus C. de Boer,* ed. Jan Krans, L. J. Lietaert Peerbolte, Peter-Ben Smit, and Arie Zwiep, Supplements to Novum Testamentum 149 (Leiden: E. Brill, 2013), 61–75. See also Gaventa, *Our Mother Saint Paul,* 113–22, where she argues that God hands humans over to the powers of Sin and Death. This is no rhetorical flourish. Speaking of the clause "God gave them up . . ." at 1:24, 26, and 28, she states: "The clause signals that the human situation depicted in Rom 1 derives both from human rebellion against God and from God's own active role in a cosmic conflict. In response to human rebellion, God surrendered humanity for a time to what we may call the anti-God powers, chief among which are Sin and Death."

20. See Martinus C. De Boer, *The Defeat of Death: Apocalyptic Eschatology in 1 Corinthians 15 and Romans 5* (Sheffield: Sheffield Academic Press, 1988), 156.

21. See ibid., 167: "For this reason, the Law's only true forensic function, also its divine purpose, is to 'work wrath' (4.15; cf. 7.1–3) and thus in effect to confirm the condemnation of Adamic humanity (5.16, 18; cf. 8.1)."

22. See Gaventa, *Our Mother Saint Paul*, 131: "This résumé of Sin's accomplishments requires something more than a generous God who forgives and forgets, and something entirely other than a Jesus who allows people to improve themselves by following the example of his good behavior. Sin cannot be avoided or passed over; it can only either be served or defeated."

23. Ernst Käsemann, *New Testament Questions of Today* (Philadelphia: Fortress Press, 1969), 109. Cf. Nancy J. Duff, "The Significance of Pauline Apocalyptic for Theological Ethics," in Marcus and Soards, *Apocalyptic and the New Testament*, 281.

24. See Beker, *Paul's Apocalyptic Gospel*, 21: "Apocalyptic, which defines the content of Paul's gospel as the hope in the coming triumph of God." See also 96–98: "the vision that God's coming triumph will transform all our present striving and sighing (Rom. 8:17–39) into the everlasting joy of his glory." See also 46: "Resurrection language is apocalyptic language: it receives its meaning from the apocalyptic hope in the resurrection of the dead, which will take place when all history finds its fulfillment in the manifestation of the apocalyptic glory of God."

25. Martinus C. De Boer, "Paul, Theologian of God's Apocalypse," *Interpretation* 56, no. 1 (January 2002): 27.

26. Richard E. Sturm, "Defining the Word 'Apocalyptic': A Problem in Biblical Criticism," in Marcus and Soards, *Apocalyptic and the New Testament*, 39: "Martyn's contribution is significant in presenting not merely the horizon of Paul's thought as apocalyptic, but even Paul's *focus* on Christ's cross/resurrection, as the heart of his gospel."

27. See ibid., 39–41; J. Louis Martyn, "Epistemology at the Turn of the Ages: 2 Corinthians 5:16," in *Christian History and Interpretation: Studies Presented to John Knox*, ed. W. R. Farmer, C. F. D. Moule, and R. R. Niebuhr (Cambridge: Cambridge University Press, 1967), 269–87.

28. Beker, *Paul's Apocalyptic Gospel*, 72.

29. Gaventa, *Our Mother Saint Paul*, 109.

30. Martyn, "Epistemology," 285.

31. Sturm, "Defining 'Apocalyptic,'" 41.

32. Martyn, "Epistemology," 286, with original emphasis.

33. Gaventa, *Our Mother Saint Paul*, 131. See also her comment on 122: "For Paul, the cross is the point at which the 'handing over' to the anti-God powers reaches its undoing, since it is here that 'God handed over his own Son' (Rom 8:31–32), which is not victory for the powers but their unmasking and the sure sign of their defeat."

34. Larry Paul Jones and Jerry L. Sumney, *Preaching Apocalyptic Texts* (St. Louis: Chalice Press, 1999), 35.

35. Martinus C. de Boer, "Paul and Apocalyptic Eschatology," in *The Origins of Apocalypticism in Judaism and Christianity*, ed. John J. Collins (New York: Continuum, 1998), 365. Rom. 8:33–34 is the same text that Gaventa cites as indicative of Paul's stress on the cross. Yet de Boer sees these verses, and thus apparently their cross emphasis, as forensic in nature.

36. Campbell, *The Deliverance of God*, 24.

37. M. C. de Boer, "Paul and Apocalyptic Eschatology," 365.

38. Ibid., 366. See also Martinus C. De Boer, "Paul's Use and Interpretation of a Justification Tradition in Galatians 2.15–21," *Journal for the Study of the New Testament* 28, no. 2 (December 2005): 215: "Paul has interpreted the atoning death of Jesus apocalyptically, as God's act of deliverance from an evil realm. For the sake of argument, Paul adopts the language of forensic-eschatological justification (in the future), but the context in which he places it forces it to take on a different meaning, that of God's rectifying power (in the present)."

39. George W. E. Nickelsburg, *Resurrection, Immortality, and Eternal Life in Intertestamental Judaism and Early Christianity* (Cambridge, MA: Harvard University Press, 2006), 229–30.

40. Beker, *Paul's Apocalyptic Gospel*, 72.

41. Ibid., 73.

42. De Boer, *The Defeat of Death*, 112.

43. Ibid., 137: "Rather, to speak of death as an inimical cosmological power is, *inter alia*, to speak of human beings as *victims* of a power they can neither withstand nor overthrow. In the case of the righteous, such victimization requires divine rectification in the form of resurrection, a resurrection that bestows life in the new age and that is strictly correlated with the overthrow and destruction of those powers that have inflicted death."

44. Stephen L. Cook, *The Apocalyptic Literature* (Nashville: Abingdon Press, 2003), 176.

45. Paul J. DaPonte, *Hope in an Age of Terror* (Maryknoll, NY: Orbis Books, 2009), 105.

46. Gaventa, *Our Mother Saint Paul*, 81–82.

47. R. E. O. White, *Biblical Ethics* (Atlanta: John Knox Press, 1979), 135.

48. This is how flesh must be understood from Rom. 7:14. Here the RSV translates *sarx* as "carnal." The NSRV gets it right: "For we know that the law is spiritual; but I am of the flesh, sold into slavery under sin." It still, though, has the sense of carnality. In fact, White recognizes that in 10 of Paul's uses of the term, he *does* speak of the desires of the flesh. References like those support the connection of Paul's use of *sarx* with the sexual meaning of "carnal" or as implying "sensual" or "sexual."

But there are other significant Pauline uses of the term that have only a remote sense of sensuality. In other places such as 1 Cor. 3:1–2, Paul uses it to refer to idolatry, witchcraft, hatred, strife, jealousy, anger, selfishness, party spirit, and envy. Then, there are other instances where no blame at all is connected with *sarx*. For example, Christian teachers may share spiritual things with their hearers. When they do, they should in return justly receive "carnal," that is, fleshly or material gifts. Paul himself talks about being present at a church meeting in Spirit, though he is absent in the "flesh," which is to say, bodily.

49. See White, *Biblical Ethics*, 137: "*Flesh* stands simply for human nature or its material side, for everything—impulses, thoughts, desires, and the like—which belongs to the outward man. . . . Flesh is simply human nature apart from God, . . . with all the limitations, moral weakness, vulnerability, creatureliness, and mortality, which being human implies." See also Rudolf Schnackenburg, *The Moral Teaching of the New Testament* (New York: Herder & Herder, 1965), 234: "Certainly the concept of *sarx* refers to the corporeal and sense-endowed character of man but nevertheless signifies the whole man in his frailty, liability to temptation, and slavery to sin. Man as *sarx* confronts God and, trusting to himself, is powerless and prone to evil."

50. See Nickelsburg, *Resurrection, Immortality*, 234: "The struggle that was ineffectual in the Flesh—the 'spiritual' character of the Torah notwithstanding (chapter 7)—is now effective through the power of the Spirit made available through the resurrection of Christ."

51. See White, *Biblical Ethics*, 138.

52. See David E. Aune, *Apocalypticism, Prophecy, and Magic in Early Christianity* (Grand Rapids: Baker Academic, 2006), 10: "For

Paul, the present time is just a temporary period between the death and resurrection of Christ on the one hand, and his return in glory on the other, in which those who believe in the gospel will share in the salvific benefits of the age to come (Gal 1:4; 2 Cor 5:17). This temporary period is characterized by the eschatological gift of the Spirit of God, experienced as present within the Christian community as well as individual believers (Rom 8:9–11; 1 Cor 6:19; 12:4–11; 1 Thess 4:8)." Also see Nickelsburg, *Resurrection, Immortality*, 234: "The Spirit dwells in Christians ([Rom.] 8:9–11), as Sin had dwelt in the Flesh, and 'leads' the children of God, as the good angel in the two-spirits tradition leads the righteous."

53. Lieven Boeve, "God Interrupts History: Apocalypticism as an Indispensable Theological Conceptual Strategy," *Louvain Studies* 26 (2001): 210.

54. Ibid., 212.

55. Ibid.

56. This quotation by King is a paraphrase of a citation made in 1853 by Unitarian abolitionist Theodore Parker. See Theodore Parker, *Ten Sermons of Religion* (Boston: Crosby, Nichols, & Co.; New York: Charles R. Francis & Co., 1853), 85. See also King's sermons: "Why I Am Opposed to the War in Vietnam," April 30, 1967, at the Ebenezer Baptist Church, Atlanta, http://www.mlkonline.net/video-mlk-opposed-to-vietnam-war.html; "Where Do We Go From Here?," August 16, 1967, at the 11th Annual SCLC (Southern Christian Leadership Conference) Convention, Atlanta, GA, http://mlk-kpp01.stanford.edu/index.php/encyclopedia/documentsentry/where_do_we_go_from_here_delivered_at_the_11th_annual_sclc_convention.

57. Duff, "The Significance of Pauline Apocalyptic," 286–87. Duff is right to mention concern for enthusiasm. Paul was certainly concerned about Corinthian enthusiasm. This concern is probably why he focused so heavily on crucifixion. But we took the cross and gloried in it. We did the unthinkable. We made the suffering man the divine man or superman. So it is not just a focus on resurrection that brings fear of glory and supersessionism.

Chapter 4: Raise the Dead

1. See http://www.maynardville.com/article/dd.htm.

2. Union Presbyterian Seminary, Richmond Campus, Richmond, Virginia.

3. David E. Campbell and Robert D. Putnam. *American Grace: How Religion Divides and Unites Us* (New York: Simon & Schuster, 2010), 146.

4. Ibid.

5. Ibid., 147.

6. Ibid.

7. Ibid., 76.

Chapter 5: Preaching Mark

1. Max Brooks, *World War Z: An Oral History of the Zombie War* (New York: Three Rivers Press, 2006), 99–100.

2. Philip Scharper and Sally Scharper, eds., *The Gospel in Art by the Peasants of Solentiname* (Maryknoll, NY: Orbis Books, 1984), 40–41.

3. Dale Allison, "The Eschatology of Jesus," in *The Origins of Apocalypticism in Judaism and Christianity*, ed. John J. Collins (New York: Continuum, 1998), 299.

4. N. T. Wright, *The New Testament and the People of God* (Minneapolis: Fortress Press, 1992), 396.

5. David Schnasa Jacobsen, *Preaching in the New Creation: The Promise of New Testament Apocalyptic Texts* (Louisville, KY: Westminster John Knox Press, 1999), 44.

6. Donald H. Juel, *The Gospel of Mark* (Nashville: Abingdon Press, 1999), 59. "The NRSV translates, 'he saw . . . the Spirit descending like a dove *on* him' (1:10). The translation is particularly unfortunate. While Matthew and Luke use 'upon,' the preposition in Mark is translated literally 'into.' Those who know Greek can appreciate why later in the story those who claim that Jesus is possessed by the ruler of demons are guilty of blasphemy against the Holy Spirit (3:22–30): Jesus is indeed possessed, but by the Spirit of God and not by a demon. Something has indeed 'gotten into him.'"

7. Ched Myers, *Binding the Strong Man: A Political Reading of Mark's Story of Jesus* (Maryknoll, NY: Orbis Books, 1988), 155.

8. Cf. Richard Horsley, "The Kingdom of God and the Renewal of Israel: Synoptic Gospels, Jesus Movements, and Apocalypticism," in *The Origins of Apocalypticism in Judaism and Christianity*, ed. John J. Collins (New York: Continuum, 1998), 342: "In addition to their differences in social location, the Gospels, particularly Mark and Q, proclaim that God's saving action, the fulfillment of the people's longings, is already happening in Jesus' preaching and practice of the kingdom of God."

9. For more on this perspective of Jesus' present ministry as a pocket of God's future revealed in the present, see the introduction in Brian K. Blount, *Go Preach! Mark's Kingdom Message and the Black Church Today* (Maryknoll: Orbis Books, 1998).

10. Juel, *The Gospel of Mark*, 163.

11. Cf. J. Christiaan Beker, *Paul's Apocalyptic Gospel: The Coming Triumph of God* (Minneapolis: Fortress Press, 1982), 87: "And unless Christians know that it is their task to establish nothing but beachheads of the kingdom of God in this world, then not only the sheer magnitude of the ethical task will suffocate them, but also their frequent inability to measure ethical progress will stifle them."

12. Donald A. Hagner, "Gospel, Kingdom, and Resurrection in the Synoptic Gospels," in *Life in the Face of Death: The Resurrection Message of the New Testament*, ed. Richard N. Longenecker (Grand Rapids: Wm. B. Eerdmans Publishing Co., 1998), 101.

13. Harlan K. Ullman and James P. Wade, *Shock and Awe: Achieving Rapid Dominance* (Washington, DC: National Defense University, 1996), 72–73.

14. Ibid., 213–17.

15. D. E. Nineham, *The Gospel of St. Mark* (London: Penguin Books, 1969), 228.

16. Cf. ibid., 225: "To persuade Jesus to shrink from these events was to tempt him to disobey the will of God, as Satan had done in the wilderness."

17. Myers, *Binding the Strong Man*, 244.

18. Raquel A. St. Clair, *Call and Consequences: A Womanist Reading of Mark* (Minneapolis: Fortress Press, 2008), 23.

19. Ibid., 139.

20. Albert Schweitzer, *The Quest of the Historical Jesus* (New York: MacMillan Publishing, 1968), 370–71.

21. Larry Paul Jones and Jerry L. Sumney, *Preaching Apocalyptic Texts* (St. Louis: Chalice Press, 1999), 33.

22. Randall W. Reed, *A Clash of Ideologies: Marxism, Liberation Theology, and Apocalypticism in New Testament Studies* (Eugene, OR: Pickwick Publications, 2010), 58.

23. Nathan R. Kerr, *Christ, History and Apocalyptic: The Politics of Christian Mission* (Eugene, OR: Cascade Books, 2009), 2.

24. Paul J. DaPonte, *Hope in an Age of Terror* (Maryknoll, NY: Orbis Books, 2009), 67.

25. Ibid.

26. Schweitzer, *Quest of the Historical Jesus*, 402.

27. Ibid., 399.

28. Sermon, "Straining Forward," preached on October 2, 2011 by Gary W. Charles at Central Presbyterian Church, Atlanta.

Chapter 6: Rise!

1. R. Alan Culpepper, *Mark* (Macon, GA: Smyth & Helwys, 2007), 183.

2. Ibid., 171.

3. M. Eugene Boring, *Mark: A Commentary* (Louisville, KY: Westminster John Knox Press, 2006), 158.

4. Culpepper, *Mark*, 177.

5. M. Eugene Boring, *Revelation* (Louisville, KY: Westminster John Knox Press, 1989), 162.

6. Culpepper, *Mark*, 177.

7. Boring, *Mark*, 162.

8. Dr. Walter W. Moore, President of Union Presbyterian Seminary from 1904 to 1926.

CPSIA information can be obtained at www.ICGtesting.com
Printed in the USA
BVOW09s2033040314

346662BV00001B/47/P